HIRE LIKE A PRO!

A Guide to Finding, Recruiting and Retaining the Best Employees

DON JASENSKY

COPYRIGHT

DEDICATION

I want to dedicate this book to my loving wife Lisa who is the most wonderful person I have ever met, and to my children Kaylie and Tyler who have inspired me and taught me more about life than I have taught them.

FOREWORD

Don Jasensky and his firm came highly recommended to me when I was looking for a CEO for one of my companies, Global Lending Services LLC. Global Lending Services was growing quickly but in a very competitive industry. We reached a point where we needed a seasoned CEO to take us to the next level and become a major player in the automotive finance industry. We retained Don and his firm and they did an extraordinary job. Don and his team went step by step, creating a job description, sourcing a group of terrific CEO candidates, assessing and evaluating the candidates. Don guided us through the interviewing and assessment process.

My partners and I were at a dilemma deciding among the group of highly qualified candidates. I remember calling Don and asking for his thoughts. He asked me one question "Which candidate has the highest ceiling?" We all immediately thought of the same candidate. The answer to this question made our decision much easier. With our new CEO at our helm, we reached our goals in just 5 years. Don and his team had the processes in place to make this search as efficient as it was effective. My team was very impressed with how thorough their processes were. I would highly recommend every executive study their processes on recruitment.

Doug Duncan,
Chairman, Global Lending Services, LLC

CONTENTS

INTRODUCTION

THE MOST IMPORTANT ingredient in your career and business success is the people you hire. They find your customers, sell your products, provide your revenue stream, solve your problems, and fend off your competition. They are your greatest asset, but their failures can be your albatross.

The problem is that you can have an MBA from an Ivy League school and still be ill-equipped to find great candidates, then interview, evaluate and make intelligent hiring decisions and keep the best on your team.

Whether you are leading a small or very large team, you will be measured by the results they produce. Your own career success depends upon the quality of the people you hire and your skill in the execution of recruitment fundamentals.

The world has changed since you started your career. The trend in the United States has moved away from the "hire for life" mentality of past generations to a much more transitory workforce. Employees are much more likely to move to another company for various reasons such as learning about a new industry, finding another mentor, possible promotion, even just to move because a new job may be more interesting. Turnover has become a constant challenge, especially with small and mid-sized companies that cannot offer promotions, pay raises, or new challenges such as moving to a different department.

Technological changes have made it much easier for workers to find new positions that seem more interesting or challenging. This has made it more difficult for companies to retain their workforce. With the advent of social media and technology, job openings are being sent to employees who are not looking, enticing your best employees. Rapid and disruptive changes in the markets can require pivots, speedy ramp-ups, and new personnel to quickly meet these challenges. Recruiting and retaining top performers has become more challenging and it looks like that trend will continue.

For you to compete in this new environment, you will need to update and build your recruiting skills. It is prudent to assume that your competitors are updating and building theirs. So the question is: Where do you go to acquire the knowledge needed to improve your recruitment skills and abilities?

A System That Works

My desire in writing this book is to share with you the recruiting system we developed to meet our client's needs, and the lessons we have learned in our 30 years of recruiting personnel throughout the United States. I want you to learn the system and techniques that we have developed and use every day in our firm so that you too can apply them to your searches.

We have successfully placed several thousand people and our searches are broad in scope. Our placements have not just been executive and senior-level searches. We have placed people at all levels of staffing, including hourly workers, technical personnel, administrative, professional, regional and field, sales, supervisors, managers and C-Level leaders.

You too may be responsible for hiring for a variety of positions at different levels in your organization. The good news is that this system works for all positions and all levels.

Our company had to learn to adapt to the changes and challenges in the marketplace, including cultural, legal, and technological shifts. Our clients pay us to produce results. We had to learn how to find, recruit, and assess candidates for all level of positions throughout the United States. Our system had to be flexible enough to evolve and adapt to the ever-changing marketplace. More importantly, our system had to produce consistent results.

In 1989, I started a personnel search firm in Lakewood, Ohio - Automotive Personnel, LLC. I started working with administrative and mid-level personnel and, as my career progressed, I moved up in the recruiting world and focused on corporate searches for upper- and C-Level hires. The involvement and intensity of hiring C-Level executives goes way beyond what I experienced years earlier filling lower-level positions. The depth to which you need to know the job, its duties and responsibilities, and where the target position can lead to in upper level positions was always both challenging and fascinating to me.

As you might expect, upper-level managers and executives are way more analytical and expect you to have in-depth knowledge of the position if you want to keep their attention. They will want to know all about the position so they can judge whether the opportunity is worth their interviewing for. They will ask you about the company, why the position is open, and about the team they will be joining, as well as the boss/mentor for whom they will be working. Their criteria for making such a decision goes much deeper than you will encounter filling an administrative position. Most recruiters cannot work at this level. That said, I was surprised to find that the essential components I learned in recruiting for lower-level positions were the same as for the senior roles.

Over the years, I have trained many recruiters and learned that I do not like hiring recruiters, I like to "make recruiters." I learned to train them to be productive on day one with our firm and to quickly spoon-feed them as they develop. This book is to memorialize what we have learned in 30 years of recruiting all levels of positions throughout the United States with the hopes of helping corporate hiring managers and business owners learn a structured system to follow for every search that will act as your "road map" leading to successful hires. Armed with this system your career will soar!

THE SYSTEM, IN SUMMARY

In this book, I endeavor to teach you the details of our system for addressing the recruitment challenges, one that is scalable and can be found in successful organizations of every size, type, and market. I want you to become the best person in your organization at recruiting, assessing, and hiring top performers. I want your career to soar as you become better at building your team. Additionally, I want you to have a system that you can teach your managers so that they too can learn and use it when they hire personnel.

In this book, you will learn the characteristics of a good recruitment system and will learn how to structure each search from beginning to the end, just like reading a road map, by understanding the components of a professional search.

Once you are armed with this proven system, your searches will be structured and make the entire recruitment process more understandable and consistently successful. You will be able to share with members of your organization a proven methodology that will make recruitment of team members easier and much more productive.

If you agree that the people you hire determine your success, then you need to do everything you can to become great at recruiting, assessing, hiring, and keeping top performers. This book is a practical guide that you can use to put in place the proven recruiting system we use at our recruitment firm every day. You too can become exceptional at recruitment and you career will prosper.

A Little Preparatory Quiz

The purpose of this quiz is to test your knowledge of the recruitment process. Take this quiz prior to reading this book and again after reading the book. See how your answers change.

1. The best indicator of a candidate's future performance and success with your organization is:

   a. How well they present themselves during your interview.

   b. They say all the things you were looking to hear.

   c. They have a strong record of successful past performance.

    d.   They aced your corporate testing.

2. The best indicator that a sales representative candidate will be a great hire for you is:

    a.   They blow you away during the interview.

    b.   You toss a stapler in their lap and ask them to "sell it to you" and they do very well selling it to you.

    c.   You see a past record of high performance.

    d.   They aced your "Profile Assessments."

    e.   If they can "sell you" during the interview they will sell to your clients as well.

3. Which point is often overlooked by employers when creating a winning job posting to attract a superior candidate?

    a.   Very detailed job description covering the duties and responsibilities of the opportunity.

    b.   List of stringent qualifications to ensure the best candidates will apply.

    c.   A description of your company and what a person can accede to in this position.

4. The best method to delegate responsibilities to hiring committees is: (Example is 5 people on hiring committee deciding between 4 candidates interviewed)

    a.   Majority rules.

    b.   Unanimous or keep looking.

    c.   All committee members have a say, but final decision rests with the member who the candidate will report to.

5. When you are interviewing a sales rep or mid-level manager, the best sign that you have a good candidate is:

    a.   Willingness to start right now with you.

    b.   Cautious, asks a lot of questions, needs time to think about it.

    c.   Blows you away during the interview.

6. Which is correct - What a candidate wants from a career move, (candidate's mindset) is:

    a.   Just as important as their education and experience.

    b.   Not your problem and should be left to the candidate to sort out.

7. Which is more reflective of a Career Seeker Vs a Job Seeker?

    a.   They come to your interview enthused and willing to jump through any hoop for you.

    b.   A willingness to commit to your position during first interview.

    c.   Wants time to reflect on your opportunity and where it will lead them.

8. Check each that apply - When interviewing candidates in-person:

    ☐ You are able to spell out a compelling reason why any candidate should consider leaving their current position to join your company.

    ☐ You can explain "what the candidate can become" by taking your position.

    ☐ You tell them about the team they will be joining.

    ☐ (If candidate is from a different industry), You have compelling reasoning for them joining your industry.

    ☐ You provide literature for candidate to take home to review and share with spouse/mentor.

9. To save everyone's time, do you prepare a list of "knock-out factors" when beginning a search such as:

    > Candidate's ability to commute to your office daily or relocate.

    > Non-compete exists that may affect their current employment.

    > Specific knowledge necessary such as "EXCEL expertise."

    > Needed licensure (driver's license needed to do job, CPA required).

    > Credit and criminal background checks needed before offer letter.

    > Ability to travel as required.

    Please note the question is not **should you**, it is **do you**...?

    ☐ Yes

    ☐ No

10. Post interview: Check all which you do regularly in your post interview meeting with your hiring committee:

    ☐ Assess each candidates' abilities to perform the needed functions of the position.

    ☐ Ask what concerns exist for each candidate.

    ☐ Ask how candidate will fit into your corporate culture.

    ☐ Ask if candidate can duplicate their past success in your position.

    ☐ Consider what obstacles candidate have in achieving the same level of success with your opportunity.

- ☐ Discuss what help – training – investment will candidate need from you and can you pay that price.

- ☐ Does candidate have a compelling reason to take your opportunity.

- ☐ What concerns does the candidate have and can you overcome them?

CHAPTER 1

CHARACTERISTICS OF A GOOD RECRUITMENT SYSTEM

S O LET'S START with the characteristics of a good recruitment system. Having worked with hundreds of companies throughout the country on several thousand successful placements, I have seen and worked with a lot of systems. This includes no system with some companies and very sophisticated systems with large firms such as Hyundai, Toyota, and

Ford. I have learned lessons from each, and this aggregate experience has taught us much.

We have seen characteristics that are consistent with all successful systems, and others that are consistent in most unsuccessful systems. In this chapter, I want to illuminate what we have learned that makes up a successful recruitment system and encourage you to consider adopting these discoveries for your organization. The need for a successful recruitment system extends from the very large organizations down to the small firms. There are some techniques that smaller firms can adopt that can make the recruitment endeavors more competitive with much larger organizations. We will share those with you.

CHARACTERISTICS OF A GOOD RECRUITMENT SYSTEM

From our experience, we have found that a good recruitment system is:

1. **Highly effective**: If you follow the system, you will consistently hire good employees who fit your open positions.

2. **Easy to use**: It is not overly complicated so that the system itself gets in the way of hiring. Your system should make the hiring process much easier, not harder.

3. **Repeatable**: It must be usable across all positions, from junior- through senior-level positions. Of course, more complex and higher-level positions require more time and effort, but the system remains the same.

4. **Teachable**: You must be able to teach the system to other employees. This is essential for a system to be

adopted as "tribal knowledge" by the employees and future employees.

5. **Easily adopted**: It must be easily adopted by new managers who join the company. A system so complex that new managers need to go off for a few days of training to learn how to use it is way too complicated and usually is abandoned unless you are with a very large company that can factor this time in for new hires.

Most large companies have a successful recruitment system, which is an important reason why they were able to grow so large. Usually these systems are managed by human resource professionals who have a formal education in, and years of experience executing, recruitment and people-management strategies. In our experience, the majority of small-through-midsize companies do not have such structured recruitment systems.

In smaller companies and in newer companies, the responsibility for hiring often falls upon the owner or department managers, such as sales managers or accounting managers. These department managers do their own recruiting, interviewing, and assessing. They may or may not have an HR manager for help. These department managers usually are great within their area — sales, accounting etc. — but have little or no structure, no training, and no proven formula to help them avoid the common hiring mistakes and make smarter hiring decisions.

With large companies, it is very different. Large companies often call for a department head to tell human resources what they need, and the human resource staff does all the work. The human resource staff presents the best candidates to the department head to interview. The department head tells HR who they like and the HR manager negotiates compensation, closes, and does the initial onboarding.

Often, the lack of a successful system causes managers to make the same hiring mistakes throughout their careers. Understand, this greatly limits their careers. Managers and executives are judged by the results their teams produce. Technical expertise and a weak team will generally produce poor results and limit your career.

Case Study: The dynamic sales manager with an anemic career

My firm was hired to help a growing consumer finance company build its field sales staff. This was a newer company that was growing quickly. I met with the their sales manager, who possessed an outgoing and dynamic personality. He showed me his very well-crafted sales training program. It all looked good — good product to sell, good leader, and a good training program. However he struggled with inadequate performance from his sales staff. The problem was with the personnel he hired.

I have seen this same problem with a large percentage of managers, especially with sales managers. Many are terrible at hiring. They are great at selling and teaching a disciplined sales system to their sales staff. However they have an ineffective or even no structured recruitment system in place and continually hire inadequate personnel. I have found that many of these managers are often very stubborn and eschew the concept of a structured recruitment system and "hire on their gut." If I only had a dollar for every time I heard a manager tell me how they go with their gut! This dynamic sales manager was consistently making this classic hiring mistake — no recruitment system in place to ensure that qualified candidates were being brought to the interviewing process, interviewed, assessed, and hired.

This mistake was holding him back from being promoted to a regional manager position. His knowledge of sales, sales training, hard work, and dynamic personality were great. However, he was overworked trying to motivate his staff, close their deals, turn around troubled deals, and always hiring new people. He was approaching burnout. How many times have I seen this scenario? How many times have you also seen it?

For several decades, I have tried to teach hiring managers that going with your gut only works after you have recruited good candidates to interview, properly assessed them, and done your due diligence on their background. A rule that we have learned is that **the best indicator of future job performance is past job performance.** Races horses love to run and plow horses like to walk. Both horses are needed but don't expect one to be successful at the other's task. We dedicate chapters in this book to how to attract terrific candidates, and how to interview and assess candidates, so that you too can learn to eliminate hiring mistakes and make smarter hiring decisions.

So what mistakes did our dynamic sales manager make and were they avoidable with a better recruiting system? He continually made the common mistake many managers make. He was hiring people who "sold him" during the interview process only to see them fizzle on the job. These are the candidates who are articulate, engaging, ask closing questions, and show a great amount of enthusiasm. They sound great and as way too many sales managers say, "Hey, if they can sell me, they can sell to anybody!"

With all these winning traits I just described, the sales manager hires them on the spot! So, why is this often a hiring disaster? After all, we can tell with our own eyes and ears that the sales candidate is articulate, engaging, asking closing questions, and even sounds enthusiastic. So allow me to tell you why it is a mistake to just go with your gut and hire this person without doing your due diligence. I want you to learn what the common hiring mistakes are and, with our system in place, avoid making them.

Having placed hundreds of successful sales representatives over the past 30 years, we have learned that there is a huge difference between **ability** to do the job and the **drive** to do it. To be successful in sales, you need both. The candidate we described above sounds like they possess the ability to do the job, but by not doing your due diligence you have no idea if the candidate possesses the drive that it takes in a competitive environment to be successful. In this case, the sales manager made a lazy decision and was only one-third of the way through the process when he made his hiring decisions. Remember that the best indicator of future job performance is past job performance. The sales manager does not know the candidates' past performance. In this book, you will learn how we do our due diligence on a candidate prior to getting them an offer from our client.

All high-performing employees can prove their success. Sales people can show you sales sheets, commission earnings, YTD earnings, and other sales data. Often they bring them to the very first interview without you having to ask. They are proud of their success and want to show you. All low-performing sales people will have excuses.

Trust but verify — Go with your gut only after you have done your due diligence. By following our system, you will eliminate hiring mistakes. Your career will soar as you build stronger teams and accomplish more. You will earn more, be promoted faster, and beat your competition both internally and externally. Plus, you will sleep easier at night knowing that your livelihood is not chained to two or three high performers who can sink you if they left. There are many high performers to choose from if you learn how to find them. I will teach you how we find them for our clients.

If this dynamic sales manager learns to take the time and effort to follow our system, he will learn the value in verifying the candidates' past performance and will arm himself with the information to make a more intelligent hiring decision. He will overcome his instinct to quickly hire someone who performs well in the interview. Learn and follow our proven system and your career will soar!

EXPECTATION DIFFERENCES IN FILLING EXECUTIVE, MID-LEVEL, ENTRY/LOWER-LEVEL POSITIONS

Our recruitment system will work equally well for any level of position, from lower-level positions to mid-level to C-Level. There are differences in the various levels and I want to highlight them here for you. Some are common sense and some are not. I want you to be prepared for them.

There is a greater level of candidate sophistication as you move from entry-level workers through senior executives. As an example, a senior-level executive will require much greater detail about a position and the financial health of a company. They will ask to see financial statements and need time to study them. Executives will openly share their concerns about your company or position. They are comfortable signing a Non-Disclosure Agreement (NDA). They will take time to assess information they learn during the interview process. Additionally, they may need several months until they can get started with your company since they may need to wait for their current contract to expire, or to finish up a complex project.

Juxtapose a senior executive's recruiting process to a lower- or entry-level candidate's. The lower-level candidate will be much less analytical and require much less data to review. Signing a NDA is usually not necessary at this level and may scare them off if you did ask them to sign it. They will more likely look elsewhere than get involved with intense or protracted negotiations. They can make a decision quickly to accept a position and usually get started in two weeks.

Here's a summary comparison:

ITEM	EXECUTIVE	MID-LEVEL MANAGER	ENTRY/LOWER-LEVEL
Level of detail about position, company, duties, and responsibilities:	Executives are very analytical and will need a great amount of detail and time to assess it all.	Will need to understand position, their manager, responsibilities and expectations.	Need to feel comfortable that they can perform the job and get along with their boss. Drive time to job is very important.
Advancement opportunities:	Very important	Often important	May or may not be important
Time frame when candidate will start with you:	2 to 4 weeks is standard; however, I have seen 6 months needed for an executive to finish an important project.	2 to 3 weeks is standard	2 weeks is standard

ITEM	EXECUTIVE	MID-LEVEL MANAGER	ENTRY/LOWER-LEVEL
Number of interviews:	Multiple, with several meetings with the boss and future co-workers.	2 to 3, sometimes these can be completed in 1 day. HR first, then hiring manager, then meet with manager's boss.	1 to 2
Amount of time needed with person they will report to:	Extensive	Moderate	Light to moderate
Negotiations:	Protracted	Straightforward and fairly quick	Basic and quick
Negotiation tolerance:	Very high, sometimes painfully high	Good	Generally weak
Length of time needed to make a decision:	Can be weeks	Fairly quick, usually within 3 days of offer letter	Very quick, sometimes agreed to at interview
Non-disclosure agreement:	Expected	Usually OK with NDA and will sign if needed	May scare them off, usually not needed
Contract – letter of intent:	Extensive and multi-paged	Letter of intent expected	May or may not expect but will appreciate
Chance of turning around a rejected offer:	Fair to good	Fair to good if you can meet their needs	Not very good but drastically improves with a generous raise in salary

I hope that I have convinced you of the vital importance of using a proven recruitment system in your organization. In our 30 years of practice, we have found six distinct components to successful recruitment systems.

In the next chapter, we will delve into the individual components that make up a professional search. These are the same components I teach recruiters who work for us.

If your system lacks one of these components, or if they are poorly executed, you are opening the door to hiring mistakes.

The 6 essential components are:

1. **Job description**
2. **Sourcing plan**: A road map to find the best candidates
   - Where to find them
   - Content and best placement for job posting
   - Databases — your own, Monster, InDeed, LinkedIn, Glassdoor, etc.
   - Networking / employee referral
   - Social Media
3. **Interviewing**: Intelligent interviewing produces intelligent hiring decisions
4. **Candidate evaluation**
5. **Offer/Negotiations/Closing**
6. **Professional onboarding**

Chapter 2

Job Description - Mine Is Different from Yours

I HAVE SEEN thousands of job descriptions from all types of companies, small through very large, from different types of industries including: automotive, banking and finance, retail, manufacturing and professional firms. One aspect they all have in common is they lack the most essential ingredients needed to help the company find the right candidate.

Typical job descriptions contain the standard: Duties – Responsibilities – Qualifications - ADA language. This gets you about halfway there. But there is very important information needed to make a terrific hire that is missing here. It is easy to find if you know what questions to ask.

Our job description is a road map leading to the right candidate for every search.

Our job description will guide:

- The content of our job posting

- Whom we select to interview

- How we present the position to candidates

- Questions that we ask during interviews and candidate assessment

- Who we hire

Here are some of the key differences in our job description I want you to add to yours:

- Description of what challenges this person will face in your position.

- Learn what problems this new employee will be expected to solve.

- What opportunities will this person be expected to leverage for the company?

- Are there any personality traits that will help employee be successful?

- Where is this person now?

- **The great question:** A year from now, what will the new employee need to accomplish to be considered a terrific hire?

Without knowing this information, we cannot find the right person for the job and we would be ill-equipped to properly assess the candidates. As an example, let's say a client asks us to find an accounting manager. This seems very straightforward doesn't it? Degree in accounting, 5 to 7 years of experience, etc. However, what we don't know is what will the accounting manager need to accomplish? Will they oversee an existing team of accountants? Build a team and spend most of their first 18 months hiring? Perhaps restructure an underperforming department and bring in proven policies and procedures?

The great question: A year from now, what will the new employee need to accomplish to be considered a terrific hire?

So why did I develop this specific question and call it the "great question"?

This question must be asked of the hiring manager and agreed to by the hiring committee. If you are working through an HR department, it is essential that this question and its answer are shared with the HR department and become the focus of what they are tasked to look for. This question gets to the heart of what this candidate will need to accomplish – not just the work they will be performing.

This great question grows in importance and the answers become more involved the higher up you go in the company ranks and with the complexity of the position.

As an example, if a recruiter is searching for a good bookkeeper, the answer to this question could be as simple as "accuracy in their work." For the controller overseeing bookkeepers, the answer can be much more complicated, such as: Establish policies and procedures that will eliminate issues with accuracy and record-keeping throughout the department, and establish training protocol for continuous improvement.

Case Study: A search for a Director of Remarketing

A client, who is an automotive finance company, needed to fill a very important position for a director of remarketing. If you are not familiar with what a remarketing department does at an automotive finance company, let me briefly explain to lend context. This department is responsible for reselling the vehicles they had to repossess. It is very important that the repossessed vehicles are sold quickly for as much as they can get for them. Important judgment decisions have to be made on how much to spend on each vehicle to recondition it, such as fixing broken glass, replacing tires, brakes, etc. Also where to send the cars to get the most money for them. A convertible Mustang may get more money in Arizona than Cincinnati. A pickup truck may be worth shipping to Texas from Chicago.

For this search, our client's human resources director emailed a job description with duties, responsibilities and qualifications for this challenging remarketing director search to us. Our client had been working on it themselves for over 120 days with no hire made. Their job description got us about halfway there. When I asked the hiring manager our "great question," in this search, the CEO immediately answered: *"More money per vehicle!" "We are leaving money on the table every month and it is driving me crazy". "Killing our bottom line."*

The CEO's answer to the great question prompted the obvious follow-up question: What's causing this? His answer got us right to the heart of the issue:

1. *Their remarketing manager was a weak leader.*

2. *They felt that they had a good remarketing staff, but they were not being held accountable for their poor numbers.*

3. *They needed someone who could **put in a system** to manage the staff and help them become more effective at their jobs and hold them accountable on a daily basis.*

4. *Better use of the auction software that is available to improve efficiencies.*

With this information, we can now identify winning candidates - let me show you how. As you can see, this most important information is not on corporate job descriptions. I want you to add this to yours.

The CEO's answer influenced our entire recruiting process, including the job posting on our own website, communications with potential candidates, interviewing, and evaluations. Allow me the opportunity to give you more depth on how the answers to the "great question" influenced our search. High-performers are always looking for more challenges that stretch them and help them grow. They also love the opportunities to apply their knowledge and experience to solve problems and leverage corporate assets. With this in mind, we presented this position to candidates as one with a terrific company with a problem. The problem was their remarketing department was underperforming and was negatively affecting the company's bottom line. We let candidates know that we needed a "Hero" to come to the rescue.

We will go into greater detail on presenting positions that get accepted. Keep this in mind – high-performers respond to a challenge. The great recruiters have learned how to accurately describe a position and appeal to these high-performing individuals. New recruiters often make the mistake many corporate hiring managers make. They are almost afraid of telling potential candidates that a position has challenges and large problems to solve. Yes, you will get many "no thank you" replies when you reach out to potential candidates. However, you will strike a chord and resonate with that high-performing employee ready for a bigger challenge. Isn't this the person you are looking for?

Our client's human resource department worked on this position for months before they asked for our help. They were a good group of corporate recruiters. However they did not ask this one key question, The Great Question, so they never really knew what to look for. They had presented numerous candidates to the hiring committee who were all rejected. We did ask "the great question" and filled the position within 30 days!

Understand the importance of what you are looking for when beginning a personnel search. Ask the Great Question!

The 1st step in executive search is understanding what you are looking for. This is often very straightforward. However, sometimes this step can be very challenging. If you have a position whereby the new employee will be one of a group doing the same work, it can be readily apparent what you are looking for.

An example of a common position we work on is for credit underwriters for banks and automotive finance companies. Credit underwriters usually join a group of other credit underwriters doing the same work. The search is to find experienced credit underwriters with automotive finance experience so that our client will not have to train the person. It is very apparent what you are searching for. We will find qualified candidates with the same title of credit underwriter from banks, credit unions, and other finance companies. Many positions are like this, straightforward and easy to understand.

What if you have a much more complex position or are establishing a new position? What if you are replacing someone and want to make changes to the existing position? This now can become much more challenging to understand what you are looking for, especially if there are other managers involved in the hiring decision. You may or may not be surprised how differently people can view what is needed for the position. If we do not truly understand the position, then how can we adequately explain it to candidates we are trying to recruit? We can't and neither can you if you do not truly understand the position and what you expect from the incumbent.

WHY THE 'GREAT QUESTION' WILL SIGNIFICANTLY IMPROVE THE RESULTS OF YOUR SEARCH!

I bet you have been in this position. You need to make an important hire. To help with the interviewing, you gather a group of employees with whom the new hire will interact. You make a list of what experience, education, and attributes each member wants to see in the candidates. A lengthy and well-intentioned job description is then created as your "checklist" for the candidates to be matched against. You are confident that the extensive search criteria will help ensure that you hire the "cream of the cream!"

After extensive interviewing, you find that the candidate you like best does not "fit all the criteria" as well as other candidates do. So you do what most commit-tees do — you hire the person who fits all the criteria, but they turn out okay at best as a contributor. How could this be if they are the one who best fit all the criteria? The answer is not readily apparent to the staff who worked so hard to produce such a so-so hire! Remember this adage – *"A camel is a race horse designed by a well-intentioned committee."*

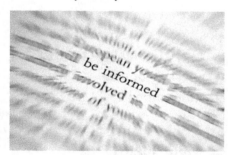Early in my career in headhunting, I realized that job descriptions were of little value to our search process. They were frequently counterproductive because clients were often "married to the requirements" and therefore passed on superior candidates (race horses) and chose candidates who pleased everyone on the hiring committees (often camels!).

I knew that I needed to find a way to "cut through" all the details of a job description and get to the **root of what was needed for success in the position**. I had to then learn how to communicate this efficiently to clients to get their cooperation so a terrific hire could be made and not a vanilla hire. I had experimented with different approaches such as questionnaires. I tried using a point system to assign weight to factors. However, in the real world where business owners and executives are so busy, these techniques got no traction. Too much added work and too complicated.

I began to ask what I now refer to as "the great question." Asking this question allows all members to focus on the aspect that is crucial to success in the position, and put correct emphasis on this as a hiring criteria. For us, it brings organization to the search process, sheds light on most important aspect of the hire, and tunes us into that little voice we call intuition.

The Great Question: *A year from now, what will a candidate need to accomplish to be considered a terrific hire?*

With this question, I have seen search committees break into arguments. That's OK!

My guidance is: "Do not give me a laundry list." Every position will have **a major focus** and everyone involved has to be on the same page. Stephen Covey taught us to "Begin with the end in mind." The great question does just that.

Case Study: Replacing an underperforming national sales manager

The Search: A mid-size subprime automotive finance company was looking to replace their national sales manager. The hiring committee gave us a long job description. As with nearly all job descriptions, there was little of value to help us hire a great candidate. The usual was included.

▶ 10 to 15 years of experience in the subprime automotive finance or consumer finance industry.

▶ College degree required.

- ▶ The CFO wanted a candidate who was very experienced with financial statements.

- ▶ The Director of Credit was on the search committee and wanted a candidate who started as a credit underwriter so that they understood the credit process and how it was affected by sales.

- ▶ The COO wanted a person who could also "assist" in the recovery area because that had been a challenging area.

- ▶ Highest score on corporate assessment tests came from HR staff.

Do you see what just happened? The request for a camel was just drawn up!

This is why it is so hard for a company of well-intentioned executives to see the mistake of this approach. They think the more the criteria, the better the candidate. The "cream of the cream" as I have heard many times. But with so many criteria — *that are not part of the root of what will drive success in this position* — they are eliminating most of the pool of candidates. They are not selecting from the best of the best; they have just greatly reduced their chances of hiring the best! This is a critical concept and a very common mistake, and I want to encourage you to take the time to think this concept through.

First, because of the multiple criteria, a much smaller group of candidates will be left to select from who meet all the criteria. There may be candidates who meet all their criteria, but there may not be a great national sales manager among them. The hiring pool shrank drastically. This is how a well-intentioned committee builds a camel! **They all mean well, but hire mediocre people.**

With so many criteria that are not part of the root of what will drive success in this position, you are eliminating most of the pool of candidates.

That is why we ask the great question — to cut through this!

Let's examine each point above.

- Of course experience is required, but setting a hard number is usually a mistake. Never be married to a number. Why? Some people are doing a better job after 3 years than others after 15 or 20 years. You need enough experience to excel at the position, but "enough" can vary greatly among candidates. Allow for this in your search. Look for accomplishments. not years.

- I love college degrees. It does show many things, such as the ability to stick with something over a long term. In many positions they are essential – director of risk, CFO, accounting, and engineering, etc. However, a degree does not correlate to being a great leader nor being driven beyond the point of personal comfort. So I will ask a client: *"If we come across a terrific NSM, and they do not have a college degree – what would you like us to do with that candidate?"* Some clients will tell us not to send any NSM candidates – regardless of how good they are - who do not have a degree. This is common with large companies. Smaller companies are usually much more flexible. Most will answer with, "Well, if they are really good and they do not have a degree, we will still be interested in them." So, why make it a hard requirement? If a client insists on a degree, that is what we will find; however, **there may be a price to pay if you will be eliminating a percentage of candidates!** This was an important point for this search. Many people attracted to the subprime automotive finance industry do not have degrees. This is just the opposite of the banking industry where degrees are expected. Perhaps this is a "nice to have" versus a "must have."

Keep this in mind: Bill Gates, Michael Dell, Mark Cuban all dropped out of college. Richard Branson (Founder of the Virgin companies) and Peter Jennings never attended college. All are exceptional leaders in their industries.

- The company's CFO wanted a national sales manager who was very experienced with financial statements. Requests like this usually stem from the fact that it may be easier to relate to someone with a similar background. However, how much experience is required? Most NSMs need to understand expenses and P&L but not opine on long-term capital projects. There is a clear difference. Depending on the company, this may be an example of a non-essential criteria adding another hump to our camel's back.

- The director of credit wants someone who worked as a credit underwriter at one point in their career to better understand the consumer credit process. Sounds good, but the problem is that most sales leaders never worked on the credit side. So you again greatly reduce your candidate pool. To put a number to this, let us say that 1 of every 10 sales managers has ever worked on the credit side. You will eliminate 90% of the candidates with this requirement. Aren't we moving away from the root of what will define success in this NSM position? Another hump added to our camel when we need to find a racehorse! I want you to start thinking like this. Without someone pointing this out to you, it is easy to make this mistake your entire career.

- COO wants someone to "assist in repossessed vehicle recovery" when needed. It is typical to add requirements to strengthen other areas of a company. Sounds great, but again how many sales managers have the ability to strengthen recovery or any other department? This is adding another hump to the camel and moving even further from the root of what a NSM will be hired to accomplish.

- Human resources focused on the highest score on their assessment tests. If you have an assessment test that has worked great for you – terrific. After 30 years of headhunting, I have not seen any tests that are a better predictor of success than looking at the candidates' proven track record or lack of it. As the great football coach Bill Parcells likes to say – " you are what your record says you are." So take the time to learn about the person's actual record. This comes from hard work and often no one on the hiring committee wants to do it.

When we asked the hiring committee the great question — *A year from now, what will the NSM need to accomplish to be considered a terrific hire?* — we quickly got to the root of their need.

Our client was getting fewer deals from its automotive dealer base because of the increased competition in their lending space. They felt pressured to fund deals of poorer quality, yielding poorer performance.

To solve this, we needed a candidate who truly understood the industry and how to raise the individual achievement of each field salesperson to make them better at selling against their competition. We needed a "hands-on " leader who would be in the field with the reps and put in a system to better train the reps and hold them accountable for their production on a daily basis.

In the end, we did not need a multi-humped camel with 15 – 20 years of experience, a college degree, vast expertise with financial statements, experience as a credit underwriter, ability to assist in recovery, nor someone to ace their corporate assessment. We needed a "racehorse" who could improve both the hunting and farming skills of the sales staff and take them, collectively, to a higher level. All racehorses have a very proven track record!

As a devotee of Stephen Covey's *The 7 Habits of Highly Effective People,* "Begin with the end in mind," and by following our system, you will be asking "The Great Question." What will the candidate need to accomplish in their first year to be considered a terrific hire? Then, focus on finding someone who can accomplish that!

We want to bring clarity to the search process and not complicate it. Time spent here answering the right questions can save you weeks in search time and will consistently lead you to the best candidates. It is very important that the hiring managers are involved with the job description. They need to discuss these questions and often they will disagree on some answers. It is important that the members of the hiring committee get on the same page so the HR staff knows what to look for and how to evaluate the candidates.

Job Description Check List

Standard
- Duties –
- Responsibilities –
- Qualifications -
- ADA language

Our additions to the Job Description

- What challenges will this person face in our position?

- What problems will this new employee be expected to solve?

- What opportunities will this person be expected to leverage for the company?

- Are there any personality traits that will help employee be successful?

- Where is this person now?

- The great question : A year from now what will the new employee need to accomplish to be considered a terrific hire?

Chapter 3

Sourcing - Your Road Map to the Best Candidate

Rule: You won't hire terrific candidates unless you are interviewing terrific candidates!

IF YOU FOLLOW our formula for creating your job description, you will discover what you are looking for and be able to communicate this to others. So now, how do you find qualified candidates?

In your management toolbox, you should have a winning formula to follow to consistently find great candidates. Let's walk through the steps of sourcing high-performing personnel that we follow at my recruitment firm. Please keep in mind we are looking for seasoned employees and not recent college graduates.

- Referrals
- Networking
- Databases
- Job Postings
- Job Fairs

Referrals

Your employees all know other people from past companies who they have worked with or may interact with at conventions and elsewhere. Ask your employees who they know who are good at what they do and are good team members. Technicians know other technicians, sales personnel worked with other sales personnel, managers know other managers. So ask employees who they worked with in the past who they thought were a good employee. We recommend having an HR staff member reach out to the potential candidate and make the call. Pay a bonus to the employee who recommended someone who leads to a hiring.

Have members of the hiring committee make a list of potential candidates they know from working together, from industry functions or groups, or by reputation. When we begin searches, we always ask if there is anyone in particular who our client wants to interview. Frequently we hear an answer such as: *Talk to the sales manager for XYZ corporation; they are leading the region with sales growth.*

Networking

Networking is how most recruiters find good candidates. We spend a lot of our time developing a vast network and dip into it with the "who do you know who can..." calls. We are talking to candidates every day and updating our own database. We attend conventions and industry events for networking purposes. Additionally, we connect with people on LinkedIn who are in our clients' industries. We join LinkedIn groups and have started our own groups to broaden our awareness. There are many industry blogs you can also join. Social media sites such as Facebook are becoming a staple for professional recruiters. We use it as a networking tool for most of our searches.

Another great networking source can be vendors who visit you, such as sales representatives selling you a product or service. They call on your competitors and often know who's who. They can be a rich source for networking. I teach my recruiters to think this way and want to encourage you to also.

Databases

Most job boards have databases you can use for a fee to find resumes. CareerBuilder, Indeed, Monster, Glassdoor and LinkedIn are well-known. It takes a lot of time to comb through these databases and find qualified candidates, time that few business owners or hiring managers have. This is often best left to your Human Resources staff if you have one.

Business owners, hiring managers and department heads are usually uncomfortable "cold-calling" and reaching out to recruit personnel they do not know. This is a very important skill that all recruiters need to master. Not everyone has the temperament or patience for this work.

If you call someone from a database, they likely will not be in the market for a new position at that time. When you do find a qualified resume, you need to know how to approach the candidate and let them know why your position is a good opportunity and what stands out about working for your company. Keep in mind that the people you are contacting already have a job, so if you simply tell them you have an opening you will not get very far. They will need to hear why this may be a better position for them. We will talk more later in the book about selling the opportunity to an employed potential candidate.

If the candidate is not interested, but you do very well highlighting the benefits of working at your company and the potential of the position, you can ask them who they know who may be interested. If your direct recruitment call goes nowhere, turn it into a networking call. Remember, combing through databases is very time-consuming and creates a lot of rejection which makes it very challenging for the caller to handle the negativity of so many "not interested" replies.

Job Postings

Job postings account for the majority of hires by most corporations. At many companies, it can account for 80% or more of their hires. We have found that higher-level positions, such as C-Level, are just the opposite. Most of the higher-level positions are filled through referrals and networking. It is very important to learn how to write successful job postings. We will go into depth on writing job postings that bring results later in this book.

Recruitment Fairs

Recruitment fairs are generally not a good place to find the seasoned, higher-level employees our clients need, so we no longer use them. However, they can be a great tool to find recent college graduates, entry-level and industry-specific personnel such as in tech or hospitality.

What we learned from our experience when we did attend career fairs is the importance of knowing who you are looking for, picking a good team to go, preparing the questions you need ahead of time, and following up quickly with the candidates you like. Invite them into your company to show them why your company is different. Also have a very nice handout about your company you can give to the people you interview at the recruitment fair. The handout should communicate what stands out about your company and why it is different from other companies they will be interviewing with.

WHAT YOU NEED TO KNOW ABOUT CREATING EFFECTIVE JOB POSTINGS

The goal of posting a position is to hire a winning candidate! So how do we do this consistently?

I want to show you how we post positions on our own website, our exclusive job board, and other job boards.

Our standard is that a posting needs to be:

- Compelling enough to
- Get attention and
- Motivate
- Terrific candidates *who are not looking*!

Why is this important to get your posting in-front of candidates not looking and how do you accomplish this?

At any given time, only a small percentage of employees are actively looking for a new position. Depending on the state of the economy, about 5% to 10% are actively looking at any given time. Those who are looking are also seeing your competition's positions. This is a slim margin to choose from!

If your job postings are just your job descriptions – duties, responsibilities and requirements, you will motivate no one.

How can you attract that other 90+% who may be open to a new position but are not looking?

Recruitment Math – a Painful Lesson!

If an employee is at a position for an average of 4 years and it

takes 2 months to find a position, then $2/48 = 4\%$ of the time an employee is looking for a new position.

This means that 96% of the qualified candidates will likely not see your posting today. Others will see it next week or next month, but you understand the point.

Keep in mind that those who are looking are seeing your competitors' postings too!

Let me show you how we increase the odds at my firm for our job postings.

Pass Along Effect: Allow me to introduce you to a concept that I stumbled across over the years. I learned that most of the candidates we place from a job posting were not looking for a position. A colleague saw the position and knew it was a good fit for their colleague and sent  it to them. This is how you reach highly-qualified candidates who are not yet looking for a position. That is why I coined the term the Pass Along Effect.

The majority of the candidates we place who came to us from a job posting had the posting sent to them from a colleague who saw it and "passed it along." These are great leads because someone from the industry determined that their colleague could benefit from the opportunity. In a sense they have been somewhat prequalified for you.

Force Multiplier: Qualified by someone "in the know." They become your salesperson and you do not even know them - if you write a compelling job posting!

It is critical to your job posting success to understand:

- How candidates conduct a job search.

- What motivates candidates to respond to a posting.

Let's discuss how job candidates look for a position. As of this writing, Google is king!

Research shows that 80% of job seekers start their job search by Googling the job title and city. Not too long ago, candidates logged on to job boards such as Monster and CareerBuilder. Now they Google and can find positions that are placed on various job boards. This is a convenience offered by changing technology. Over 60% start a search on their phones and tablets.

So job postings must be Google-friendly. You need to understand the three filters Google uses when they are applying ranks to job postings. If you do not know what they are, the best-written job postings will not be seen. What are these magical ingredients and can they allow a small company with a limited budget to compete?

Good news is it is very easy to incorporate these aspects into your job postings. My caution to you is that it is also very easy not to incorporate them, which will greatly weaken the readership of your job posting. These filters Google uses may be massaged or change in the future.

Here are the 3 things you need to incorporate to maximize Google ranking:

- Job title

- Salary

- City or zip code

The Job title needs to be clear and direct. Such as Field Sales Representative or Software Developer. I was taught years ago when we advertised in newspapers to use "eye-catching terms" such as Top Guns only for sales people, or Software Guru for a Software Developer. Those worked well in the day when newspapers or trade magazines were the predominant medium. In the age of Google, this is no longer the case. Google ranks your posting and this is a filter they use. Use clear, commonly used titles.

Job boards often have a drop down box where you enter the job title, offering a list of commonly used terms. Let me highly encourage you to use them. There is a place for creativity in job postings, but not in selecting job titles for online postings.

Google puts more weight on postings that include salaries or hourly wages. I understand that most companies do not want to list compensation in their ads, but be warned that there is a price to pay if you do not – Google will give you a lower placement ranking, and who is king?

These 3 elements **need to be in your job posting** to get adequate placement in the listing Google will present. Additionally, adding a street address will also give your posting a higher ranking on a Google search because Google likes to give directions on a map. They can generate income with this advertising and collect valuable data about the people who click on your job posting.

Advertising Content

Smart Recruitment Rule: High-performing employees do not leave for just another job; they leave for a better job.

Your posting should assimilate the ingredients high-performing employees seek in a **"better job"** to motivate candidates to answer your job posting. In our 30 years, this is what we hear most from high-performing candidates about what they value most as they look to make a job change:

- Challenge
- Company
- Team – including their boss/mentor and their peers
- Ability to advance their career

Let me encourage you to incorporate these ingredients in your job postings. This is where your creativity can be utilized. Let's briefly go over theory, then discuss some actual postings.

Challenge can mean different things to different people. To one person, it may mean taking a department and raising the bar to a higher level of performance. To another, it may mean taking on a disaster and fixing it or starting something new. Another person may want to move up to the next level such as a supervisor, move into a manager position, or a regional person to move to corporate. The commonality is high-performing employees are looking for a position that will stretch them, so describe the challenge the new employee will be taking on in your posting. Amateur recruiters often avoid talking about the challenges the new employee will be tackling. This is why they remain amateurs. However, this is not you; you are learning how to recruit high-performers.

A **better company** can also mean different things to different people. A better company may mean stable ownership to one person, while another may be seeking a high-risk exciting startup. To one person, it may be a larger company with more assets to utilize, to another it may mean a smaller company where they can see the impact of their hard work. Assume the reader of your job posting knows nothing about your company. Tell them about your company, its philosophy, mission or values, and why is it a terrific place to work. This is how our job postings get attention and are worthy of being "passed along" to colleagues. Unless taught by a seasoned professional how to post a position, most people write postings that give just the duties, responsibilities, qualifications, and ADA language. They motivate no one. Sadly, without mentoring they will repeat this mistake throughout their career. Not you, you will not be making this mistake anymore.

The **team** is very important to high-performing employees. Younger employees are often looking to join a group that can help them grow, with a leader to mentor them. Seasoned employees often are looking for a younger group to mentor so they can impart the wisdom they have accumulated. Include information about the team in your job postings and why they are an awesome group to work with.

The **ability to advance a career** is the key motivator for many high-performing employees. Make sure your job posting explains how a candidate can advance their career. Sometimes it is taking on additional responsibilities; sometimes it is preparing an employee for a higher level

GROWTH & DEVELOPMENT

position. For some positions, it may be paying for their required certifications so the employee can advance in their role. In your job posting, take the time to tell candidates how they can advance their career in your position and you will attract higher-performing candidates!

So now that we know how candidates search and what they are looking for, let's learn how to package this so you can create effective job postings that will beat your competition!

If Don Draper from Madmen were here, he would tell you to get their attention, make them want your product and then tell them go get it!

The classic foundation of advertising – AIDA

The key elements are:

- Attention
- Interest
- Desire
- Action

Attention

The primary tool here involves a headline with a supportive sub-headline. For your headline to be Google-friendly, it needs to be a known title such as sales manager or director of sales. Creative titles were popular in years past, such as collection wizard or sales guru, however they are no longer good practice because they are not Google friendly and Google is king.

Your "sub-headline" can be a creative attention getter such as "Dream Job" or "Come grow with us" or " Industry leader."

Sub-headlines lend color and flavor to your ads and can be an emotional pull to read on if written well. I will give you examples with actual ads we have used.

Interest

Use language describing your company, position, and team to tell the story of your company. Unless you are a "brand name" company, Ford, Apple, Kohl's, McDonald's, the reader may not even know who you are. Keep this point in mind, that the reader does not know why you are a terrific place to work. So tell them about your company, your mission, corporate philosophy and values in your posting and the reader will be much more likely to respond or "pass it along" to a colleague.

Desire

High-performers want to join a winning team. They respond to challenges that stretch them, so tell them what challenges they will face and what corporate assets can be better leveraged. High-performing employees are looking for day-to-day work content that will be interesting, rewarding, and help them grow. Talk about these in your job postings and you will motivate the high-performers to respond.

Please note, I am not suggesting you list all the issues the company has in your job posting. I want you to talk about the specific challenge that the hired employee will tackle. Remember what motivates high-performers – challenge!

Action

You got their attention, built interest, and desire; now tell them what you want them to do next. Do you want them to call, email a resume, fill out an online application or come by in person?

On the next few pages, we'll look at three actual job postings that we have placed successfully on our website and our own job board. Our clients fill all types of positions, so we want to cover a range of positions here for your knowledge.

First is for an hourly worker – automotive technician, then an executive, and lastly, a sales representative. I want you to notice how the ads are all similar, incorporating Attention, Interest, Desire, and Action.

Follow this proven formula that we have developed and you too can greatly improve the results of your job postings!

AUTOMOTIVE TECHNICIAN!
Is this your dream opportunity?

What makes this a dream position: ← **Great attention-getter**

- Great family ownership treats employees with respect
- Family-friendly hours – no nights and a 5-day work week **Building interest & desire**
- Paid overtime and plenty of work!!!
- Several service bays per Tech
- $18 to $30 per hour

Come by and meet the team, see for yourself! ← **Make it easy for them**

Busy automotive service center is growing and seeking experienced Auto Technicians. You will be working in a modern service facility and joining a terrific team! Work with small group of dedicated Automotive Technicians in very professional environment.

- great work environment
- terrific facility **Building desire**
- convenient location Bedford, Ohio
- plenty of work!

We are seeking ASE Certified Technicians with good references and the ability to work well with other team members. Valid driver's license needed for shop insurance coverage.

Position will pay top dollar per hour plus overtime plus monthly bonus that can reach an extra $2500! Come on by, see the facilities and talk to the Service Manager. Meet the team! Bring a colleague with you!!!

If you – or a colleague of yours – is interested please call Beth in total confidence at: **Prompt for 'Pass-along'**
Automotive Personnel, LLC (Phone number here)
name@automotivepersonnel.careers www.automotivepersonnel.careers **Call for Action**

Automotive Personnel, LLC is in its 30th year placing personnel with automotive service departments!

KEY WORDS: automotive repair, automotive service, auto technician, mechanic, Bedford, Ohio

DIRECTOR OF REMARKETING – AUTOMOTIVE FINANCE !
Growing company with unique opportunity

Our client is a well-established automotive finance company. They provide a professional work environment and an opportunity to grow your career. We have been retained to help them find a Director of Remarketing. This is a unique opportunity to join a growing subprime automotive finance company and be part of a team of dedicated industry professionals. Position reports directly to the President.

We are seeking candidates who respond to challenge and possess the commitment to "continuous improvement". Our Director of Remarketing will take on the challenge of improving dollars recovered on vehicles assets to industry standards in their 1st 6 months then raise the bar to performing better than industry standards over the next 6 months.

Appeal to challenge and build desire

To accomplish this we are looking for a Remarketing leader with a proven system they can put in place. Additionally they will need to have the ability to lead a staff of Recovery and Remarketing team members and teach them how to be more productive and effective in their day to day work efforts. You will be inheriting a good team that needs leadership, training and accountability.

Responsibilities will include overseeing all aspects of asset remarketing through the auto auctions and online sales. Managing relationships with all auctions and maximizing asset value is central to success in this opportunity.

DUTIES AND RESPONSIBILITIES:
- Responsible for processing all remarketing activities including processing title work, dealer and auction assignments, negotiating fees, setting bids, accepting bids and securing recovery payments.
- Evaluate condition of repossessed vehicles and authorize reconditioning per company policy
- Coordinate efforts with dealers and auctions to expedite disposal of vehicle.
- Value vehicles and set minimum sale amount
- Negotiate, verify and document all fees with dealers and auctions
- Provide weekly and monthly reports on current status of vehicles within the remarketing portfolio.

To help ensure a great fit for both the candidate and the employer, we are seeking candidates with the following experiences / skills / abilities:
- Vehicle remarketing experience from bank, finance company or auction
- Ability to negotiate with auctions and eliminate unnecessary fees
- Excellent verbal and written communication skills required
- Ability to travel up to 50% of work week to auctions in multiple states
- Ability to solve practical problems and deal with a variety of variables where stressful situations may exist (auctions can be busy and loud)
- It is required to have multi-tasking and proven organizational skills
- Requires the ability to be a team player and communicate well with employees in other areas and departments and with customers
- Must be familiar with Windows environment
- Requires a sense of urgency regarding time-sensitive matters as well as accuracy regarding details and data
- Flexible schedule and shift work may be required
- Ability to commute to Atlanta metro area

Prompt for 'Pass-along'

If you – or a colleague of yours – is an experienced Remarketing leader interested in a new opportunity with a growing company, we would like to talk with you in confidence. Executive compensation including starting salary $150 to 180K plus bonuses and corporate benefits. Please contact Don from Automotive Personnel, LLC 216-226-8190 don@automotivepersonnel.careers www.automotivepersonnel.careers
Automotive Personnel, LLC is in its 30th year serving the automotive industry !

Call for Action

KEY WORDS: Remarketing, automotive finance, subprime automotive finance, asset recovery,

SALES REPRESENTATIVE

If you are seeking an exciting career in a growing company and booming industry then we may have your dream position! **Attention-getter**

Our client is a very successful and growing automotive dealership.We are seeking candidates who like a fast-paced day with the ability to interact with all types of people.

Day to Day Responsibility for Sales Representative:

Expect several hours per day phone work – following up on customers - cold calling / prospecting new customers. Meet with customers at dealership, develop a credit profile of the customer, and establish what type of vehicle and payment they are qualified for. Demonstrate and show vehicle, close deal, and assist with financial paperwork.

You will be working in a highly structured, proven sales program designed to monitor your key activities and lead you to repeatable success. You must be comfortable with sales meetings, sales reporting, filling out forms, and logging work activity. The corporation will spend time and money training you and teaching their successful formula. **Building interest**

It is important to understand that you need to learn and follow their system. This will help ensure your success. If you do not like a highly structured sales program then this would not be a fit for you.

Qualifying for an acceptable "mind-set"

Our client is looking for candidates with the following experiences / traits / abilities:

- experience with retail sales, customer service, B2C commissioned sales is a natural fit
- experience as a Collector or similar position where you initiated contact with the public is a good fit
- very professional and courteous demeanor
- desire and commitment to make 60K+ yearly
- enjoy meeting with and talking to customers
- organizational skills
- computer literate
- ability to work retail hours
- ability to work in / commute to Melbourne, FL

Position provides a generous monthly guarantee, bonuses, commissions and benefits and a very professional work environment where you will be treated like a professional .

If you – or a colleague of yours - have the above experience and desire a rewarding and exciting career, please contact Don at Automotive Personnel, LLC for a confidential interview Don@automotivepersonnel.careers 216-226-8190

Automotive Personnel, LLC is beginning its 30th year serving the automotive industry !

KEY WORDS: retail sales, commissioned sales, automotive, retail, Melbourne, Florida

Talking to Candidates

Most recruiters and human resource personnel find this to be the best part of their day. Talking to candidates is way more interesting than reading resumes on a computer screen. However, I cannot say the same for business owners or department heads who have to take these calls.

If you are accepting candidate calls responding to your job postings, they can and do come at times where you may be immersed in another project. For this reason, most companies do not put in phone numbers. Most companies ask candidates to send a resume or apply online. This allows you the opportunity to read through the resumes and make calls at your convenience. This is a common and acceptable practice.

The downside to this approach is that many qualified candidates are "interested in hearing more" but not ready to formally apply. Many want to talk to someone to gather information to decide if they want to apply. At my recruitment firm, every job posting has the phone number for the recruiter to contact as well as their email. We have placed hundreds of terrific candidates over the years who were not ready to make a move, but our posting or other communication to them aroused their curiosity enough to call and hear more about it. That's the intent of a well-written posting isn't it? However, if you do not have the trained staff with the time for and appreciation of these incoming candidate calls, then have candidates email a resume or apply online, or turn it all over to a professional recruitment firm.

Let me share some thoughts on what we have learned when you are discussing your position with potential candidates. For this exercise, you are discussing the position on the phone and not in person. The candidate replied to your job posting or could have been referred to you. Maybe you have several different positions you are recruiting for.

Be prepared; calls from potential candidates can come in at any time during your workday. They can and do come in when you are in the middle of another task and you have to quickly get into the "recruiter mode" to have a professional call. I have my recruiters create highlight sheets for each position they are working on and keep it on their desks. We use these to make sure that they can discuss the position accurately and not have to rely on memory.

Please remember that you are discussing this position with an individual, a human being. Make your calls personable. These calls are not a disruption if they are part of your job. It is easy for a very busy business owner or department head who is taking these calls to get frustrated because they are answering a bunch of questions for a person who they do not know, and don't know if they are even qualified for the position. It is better if you have a dedicated HR staff member taking these calls. Of course, all large companies have the dedicated HR staffing. However, small companies, startup companies, and many mid-size companies may not. I want you to be prepared if you are accepting these calls.

Whether calls are inbound from the candidate, or outbound by you, these calls are not an interrogation on your part. They are a two-way conversation. Our natural business instincts are to qualify the candidate immediately. You do need to qualify the candidates, but do it tactfully. You want to get off the phone quickly and respectfully with an unqualified candidate.

However, the common mistake people make here, and one I want you to avoid, is turning off qualified candidates, which is easy to do. As soon as I know a candidate is not qualified, I want to disengage from the conversation. With unqualified inbound calls, I often tell the candidates to send me a resume that I can read through and I tell them will get back with them if it meets my client's criteria. I will read their resume and call them if they are qualified for this or possibly another position.

During these calls, whether I am initiating the call or taking an inbound call, I keep in mind the factors that we discussed earlier that motivate high-performing candidates: Challenge, company, team and ability to advance their career. I like to weave these into the discussion.

Sample call for our Remarketing Director posting:

Start the call correctly by keeping it conversational and informative. Have your highlight sheet on your desk and use it as a guide. Do not read it to the candidate, it is better used as a checklist. The call can go in many directions, let's make sure you start it off correctly.

> **Candidate:** I saw your posting and would like to know more about it.

> **Recruiter:** Thank you for calling. My name is Don Jasensky. What is your name?

> **Candidate:** My name is Bob Thompson.

> **Recruiter:** Good morning/afternoon Bob. I am working on several opportunities, which one are you calling about?

> **Candidate:** The Remarketing Director in Atlanta.

Recruiter: Sure, let me get that folder and tell you about the opportunity. While I am getting that out Bob, tell me what appealed to you in the - (job posting - or email) from us. (Their answer will tell me a lot about them early in our conversation).

Candidate: I have been in automotive remarketing for 12 years now and am looking for a new challenge. I am at a good place in my career where I can make a change.

Recruiter: Twelve years, that's great. (I like to start with a compliment, helps people relax and open up and is respectful).

Recruiter: Bob tell me what you what you have been doing the past half dozen years in automotive remarketing? (I ask this way for several reasons. If I don't emphasize the last half dozen years, many candidates start 20 or 30 years back in their first job out of school. I do not have an interest in all that at this point. Amateur recruiters will waste 20 minutes listening to a well-intentioned candidate go through 30 years of needless details. I want to know if they are working at the level my client needs. Perhaps this candidate has 12 years automotive remarketing as a single contributor role. My client needed a seasoned leader over a large team, that would not be a fit for my client.)

If I do like their background.......

Recruiter: Bob, let me tell you about the position...

As I explain the position, I discuss the challenges and the changes we need the remarketing director to make in the department. This will turn off candidates not up for the challenge, but will turn on the candidates looking for more challenge. That is exactly what you want to do at this point. These are the high-performers we are looking for. I will talk about the company and why it is a terrific place to put their career. This is especially important for companies that are smaller or not well-known. You are at your company 40+ hours per week. Sometimes you need to be reminded that the person you are interviewing may not know anything about it. This is your reminder!

Early in my headhunting career, I built a practice working with automotive dealerships in Cleveland, Ohio. As with most other major cities, we had a mix of some huge automotive dealer-ships and many smaller ones. The huge ones had very large advertising budgets and were on TV, radio, billboards, and newspapers. Everyone in the area knew of them. The smaller dealerships had limited advertising budgets and were not well-known outside of their immediate trade area. Who do you think received the most job applications? Of course the large, well-known dealerships did. The smaller stores may be great places to work but had a very difficult time attracting candidates. This is true of startups and smaller companies. Remember the old African adage: When elephants do battle, the ants get crushed!

I also discuss who the person will be reporting to. This is a very important criteria for high-performing candidates. In this case, the remarketing director will be reporting directly to the President. I use this as a selling point and describe how well-respected the President is in the industry. What a wonder-ful mentoring opportunity to be reporting to a person who has ascended to this level. I want you to think this way too.

Who you report to means a lot to your "career visibility." The higher up the command chain you report to, the greater for your career visibility. This appeals to another key decision criteria used by high-performers — ability to advance their career.

You may also be filling positions for candidates not moving up the corporate ladder, such as technical personnel. They may be more interested in knowing that their "boss" is a fair and decent person and will treat them respectfully. Discuss this with the candidates. Even if they are not looking to move up the corporate chain of command, who they will be reporting to and working with every day is very important to them. I want you to understand these calls at a deeper level and know how to weave these components into your interviews and use them as selling points.

CHAPTER 4

INTELLIGENT INTERVIEWING

SMART RECRUITMENT RULE: INTELLIGENT INTERVIEWING PRODUCES INTELLIGENT HIRING DECISIONS!

MOST CLIENTS TELL us that they often feel uncomfortable starting an interview. You will feel much more comfortable if you prepare intelligent questions ahead of time, and good reference checking and "due diligence" ahead of the interview will help you prepare the question that can get to the heart of the candidate's prior performance.

The objective of interviewing is fact-finding so that you can accurately assess a candidate. Here is what we look for in the interviewing process:

- Proven performance

- Would they excel in your position?

- Do they possess the traits we look for in high-performers?

- Do you have the time/capacity/ability to provide any needed training?

- Cultural fit

- Knock-out factors such as a non-compete, spouse won't relocate, bad attitude.

Smart Recruitment Rule: Prepare your questions ahead of time. Make them real-world questions that will yield information to help you make intelligent hiring decisions.

▶ What are the performance standards for your current position?

▶ How are they measured?

▶ How are you doing with them?

▶ **Show Me**: Can you provide information to support this? (performance appraisals, commission sheets, awards)

▶ References: Can you provide references who can verify your success?

▶ How would you rank your job performance on a scale of 1 to 10?

▶ What do you need to do to take your performance to the next level?

▶ How are you doing with that?

By asking real world questions, explaining your situation and discussing it with the candidates is how you really get to interact with the candidates just as you will if they were your employee. You will learn how they think and get a sense if they can solve your problem or run your department.

Here are several position-specific questions we commonly ask after describing what needs to be resolved by the new employee.

Real world questions
Explain your situation then ask ...

- Have you been in a similar situation in your career?

- Do you think you could fix that?

- What reports/data would you need from us to resolve this problem?

- Walk us through the steps to fixing this.

7 components to ensure that you are hiring a terrific candidate

Over the past 30 years in executive search and several years as a general manager at a dealership prior, I have found 7 components common to all terrific hires. We focus on these components when we are evaluating candidates and I want to share them with you. Hopefully this helps give focus to your searches.

I want you to think of your best hires and then your worst hires. Think about these components and see if your best hires had them and if one or more of the components were missing in your worst hires. If you know what you are looking for ahead of time, your searches will have more direction and you will have much more confidence in your decision making.

1. **Competency:** Is the candidate good at what they do? Are they a high-performer? The best indicator of future behavior is past behavior. Winners show themselves early and consistently throughout their careers.

2. **Capacity:** Do they have a high enough ceiling for the new position? A "rock star" sales representative needs an additional skill set to be a sales manager. Often moving from a manager level to a VP level with a company means the candidate will need to transform from focusing on tactical thinking to add strategic thinking to be successful. Are you looking for this in your candidates?

3. **Teammate Factor:** Are they naturally looking out for the overall good of the company and colleagues, or are they the one complaining at the water cooler about management, pay, working conditions, etc. It is difficult to have a "bad attitude" and still be a good team player. Fundamental to being an exceptional teammate is good

character and integrity. Don't overlook this component; a technically competent employee who is always stirring the pot is a problem!

For leadership roles and high-level single contributor roles add:

4. **Drive / Initiative:** It takes enormous energy to grow and lead a team, department or a company. Low-energy people can be competent, but they will not build or grow your company.

5. **Motivate others to achieve higher results consistently:** You cannot lead if you cannot motivate others. Many mid-level managers are technically competent, but lack the ability to energize their staff and drive higher results through them.

6. **Judgment/Decision making:** Are they consistently working on the right problems? Do they get to "root causes" of problems. Are they looking ahead and anticipating future challenges and opportunities? Do they understand how to both leverage and protect the assets of your company?

7. **Resolve:** Can they consistently see very challenging projects through to their conclusion? Sudden changes in business, competitive field, economic factors are very challenging and personally impact team members and can sometimes take years to successfully resolve. Initiating a large project and seeing it through to conclusion require two different personality types. Deciding to start a large project is more about initiative; seeing it to conclusion is more about resolve.

How does this compare to your list? Most of the clients who have hired us do not have such a list. This is true of both large and small companies. I want to encourage you to have your own list and hope our list is helpful to you.

ADDITIONAL INTELLIGENT QUESTIONS THAT YIELD RESULTS

If we are looking for drive, ability to motivate others, judgment and resolve ask for examples.

- **Initiative**: Can you give me a couple of examples of where you initiated somethings that benefited the company?

- **Drive/Ability to raise the bar**: We need someone who can raise the bar. Tell me about your team and how they are performing and how you specifically improved them.

- **Judgment:** For this position, we need someone who can make good decisions. Let's talk about several examples of where you showed terrific judgment / decision making

- **Resolve:** Ours is a tough and very competitive business. Can you give me a couple of examples of where you showed great resolve ?

Ending the 1st interview like a Pro!

If we like the candidate at the end of the interview, we try to accomplish these 3 things:

1. Gauge their interest level.
2. Ask for their concerns that we need to resolve.
3. Keep their compensation requests in line.

"We are interviewing some terrific candidates, but I don't mind telling you that I think you would do very well here. Before we finish this interview, please tell me your thoughts and any concerns you may have."

This is the time to find out if your candidate has any concerns that you can respond to before they go home misunderstanding something. In the event that the candidate decides to decline your position based on a misunderstanding about the position, it can be very difficult to get them to revisit the opportunity, especially if their spouse was involved. Now you have two people who need to change their decision.

Additionally, letting them know that you are interviewing other qualified candidates often influences their demands on salary if they know there is competition for the position. You will have to pay fair market rate to attract good employees. You will likely have to pay well above fair market rate if your candidate believes that they have no real competition for the position.

Follow-up interviews

Second interviews and follow-up interviews are the times to fill in any gaps you still need to learn about the candidate and confirm what you learned in the first interview. I highly recommend a checklist of questions to ask prior to the interview. Be open-minded and prepared to change your mind about the candidate with additional information. You may like a candidate more after their second interview or you may learn something that disqualifies the candidate. Second interviews also commonly change the ranking of candidates being interviewed. After the first round of interviewing 5 candidates, you will have a mental ranking of the candidates. This ranking usually changes with additional interviews.

Second interviews are the time to get deeper into how the candidates think, to learn about their philosophy on management and leadership, and how they resolve problems. At this point, the candidates know about your position, your company and problems to resolve. More importantly, they will have had more time to think about and reflect on what they have learned. High-performing candidates will use this interview to delve deeper into how they will work, manage their new team, solve your problems, and better leverage your opportunities. They will have better-formed and more in-depth answers to your questions. If you are prepared, you will learn a lot more about each candidate to help make an intelligent hiring decision.

Second and other follow-up interviews are crucial to the assessment process when filling positions where the candidate will be expected to solve problems and make judgment decisions. Since they will know more about situations that they will need to manage or fix, your discussions will be a setting similar to what you will have if the candidate joins your team. If you use the questions I presented earlier, you will be solving actual problems with the candidate. You, your hiring team, and the candidate will come away with a greater sense of how well you work together or not.

This is when you can observe and learn how candidates will actually solve problems. These second interviews, for me, are conducted more like you are collaborating with a team member. I want to learn if I like working with this person and how they will mesh with the team. Their personality and temperament will also show itself if you are a skilled interviewer. If you use real-world questions like these, you will eliminate most hiring mistakes.

Expect that the candidates will also have additional questions. It is common for managers and executives to ask for financial data and performance data so that they can better understand what they will be getting into and what it will take in terms of time and effort and dollars to get there. We often have candidates sign a Non-Disclosure Agreement (NDA) prior to our clients sharing corporate data not available to the general public.

Panel interviews

Panel interviews generally consist of 3 to 6 interviewers meeting with a candidate at the same time. They are not used as often for lower-level individual contributor roles but are a staple of mid- through senior-management positions. They are also common for a higher-level individual contributor role such as a corporate attorney and account executive and senior sales roles.

Panel interviews work well for several reasons. There is less stress on the interviewer because the interviewer has other team members there too. This allows interviewers time to think about a candidate's answer and reflect upon it instead of immediately asking the next question. This opportunity to be more of an observer is very important to truly understanding the candidate you are interviewing. Panel interviews are not as personality-based as one-on-one interviews. This helps eliminate personality biases when interviewing.

Panel interviews are often arranged to save time. Instead of an all-day interview, you can usually conduct a great panel interview in less than two hours. If you like the candidate, then one-on-one or two-on-one interviews or lunch with the hiring manager usually follows after the panel interview. I have found in my 30-years-plus experience that top candidates enjoy panel interviews. It gives them a chance to shine.

Allow me the opportunity to share what I have learned for conducting successful panel interviews.

- First, this is not an interrogation.

- The more comfortable the room is, the more productive the interview will be.

- You want the candidate comfortable because they will be more open and provide you a more accurate picture of themselves.

- Each interviewer should have an objective and prearranged questions to make sure you can collect all the information necessary to make an informed and intelligent hiring decision.

- Depending on the team interviewing, it is usually helpful to assign a leader who will start, moderate, and end the interview.

- Let the candidate know the format a few days prior to the interview.

- I like to prepare talking points to share with the panelists and candidates. This often includes deeper-level questions, such as how they would solve a problem, trends in the industry that they see, examples of their accomplishments, and how they achieved them, their management style, and philosophy on leading others.

- Some of our clients give candidates a homework project relating to the business and use it as fodder for an in-depth discussion.

- You will turn off good candidates if the panel adopts an "attitude of superiority." You know what that means; it's the attitude that we ask the questions and give up little information. This isn't an interrogation nor a poker game. It is a two-way street allowing both parties to gather the information and make intelligent decisions.

Please don't be this group!

Not this group!

This is more like it

I'm poking fun at panel interviews with two of these pictures, but as much as I like a well-run panel interview, I have seen teams poorly put together and attitudes that are reflected in these pictures. Always be respectful of candidates, even those who are interviewing poorly.

Case Study: The arrogant giant bank

In the late 1990s, we were contacted by one of the largest banking enterprises in the country, if not the world. Their employees certainly had every right to feel a great sense of pride to be a part of such a successful organization.

However there was a very strong sense of arrogance with this bank. They wanted to expand their work with automotive loans and wanted to work with automotive dealers. This is called indirect auto finance since the bank works indirectly through automotive dealerships to generate the loans. The dealership's Finance and Insurance (F&I) Manager talks with the customer after the sales person closes the deal. The F&I Manager does all the arrangement for the loan. If you bought a car at a dealership, you talked to their F&I Manager.

This huge bank wanted us to help them find field sales representatives to call on and enroll automotive dealers in their indirect auto loan program. Great work for us and right in our wheelhouse. I remember when that call came in. The arrogance was so unnecessary and such a turn-off. Here is how the call started.

Bank: This is (executive's name) from (name of bank). I won't waste my time asking if you know who we are. We are expanding our automotive indirect lending where we will become the dominant player in the industry. We are contacting you and many other recruitment firms around the country — and there are a lot of you out there — to help us find field sales representatives.

Me: That is great, thank you for thinking of us.

Bank: Get a pen. Write this down. Dollar sign. The number 3. A comma. A zero. Another zero, another zero. A comma. Now write down another zero. Add another zero. Add another. Add another comma. Now add another zero. Add another zero. Add one more zero. Add a comma, another zero, another zero add one more zero. That's three trillion in assets, that's who the hell we are. Now who are you and why am I even talking to you?

This put-you-in-your-place controlling language was both unnecessary and a huge turn-off. I made a decision during this call that we will use the company as future hunting grounds for our clients and not do business with this bank. If you are with a well-known brand, that's great. Don't use that as an excuse to talk down to candidates. Always be respectful to candidates. They may be with a much smaller company but they still have pride in their accomplishments.

Chapter 5

Candidate Evaluation and Assessment

POST INTERVIEW - How to Make Smarter Hiring Decisions

So you have several good candidates. Perhaps members of your hiring committee are split as to whom you should hire. Let's bring clarity to the evaluation process so you can cover all your bases and make a smart hiring decision.

After the interviews, ask yourself and members of the hiring team about each candidate. Have a list of talking points that will help organize and lead to **intelligent conversations** about each candidate. This will help bring clarity to your decision.

Let's review what you are looking for in the evaluation phase of recruitment:

- Proven performance

- Strengths and weaknesses of each candidate

- Would they excel in your position and duplicate their past success?

- Motivation

- Do you have the time/capacity/ability to provide adequate training?

- Cultural fit

- Knock-out factors such as a non-compete, spouse won't relocate, bad attitude, integrity issue

Make sure someone is in charge of the reference-checking and reports back to the hiring team. The references should help confirm a candidate's contributions, work style, promotions, and achievements.

Caution: Most candidates can sparkle in the interview and really talk Xs and Os. However when you are looking for an initiator, a business driver who can sustain success, that is much harder to find. Talk the talk vs walk the walk. You have to research their past performance to know this. Check with their references and dig into what the candidate accomplished.

TIP: I hear from managers and executives that references are often worthless because people are reluctant to talk about a candidate. This is easy to overcome if you know how. A favorite technique of ours is to tell the candidate to call each reference and let the reference know it is OK to talk to us. We have found that if candidates call their references and give them their okay to speak openly with us, we get much more helpful information on a candidate than calling them cold. But this is very time-consuming and often overlooked by hiring committees. Follow our system and you will never make this mistake again!

Proven performance

A rule of personnel recruitment is: " The best indicator of future performance is past performance." Human behavior follows patterns throughout our adult life. High-performers tend to distinguish themselves early in their careers and throughout. Lower-performing employees also have a history trail. In the candidate evaluation phase, we focus our mental capital on dissecting the information gathered during the interviews, testing, and reference-checking so that we can make an intelligent hiring decision based on facts.

"From – To" questions are good here. Sales Manager grew profitability from $X to $X+ or a Controller reduced closing from 4 days to 3 days.

Throughout my career, I have heard many hiring managers state: "I go with my gut." I certainly understand this sentiment. We learn to rely on our ability go with feelings instead of researching the facts. Let me suggest this, go with your gut only after you have done your research and reference checking. There is no excuse to not do your homework on a candidate. It

may seem time-consuming to conduct multiple interviews, check references, discuss the candidates with your hiring committee – and it is. **Let me suggest that all this is a lot less work than making a bad hire will be! Remember this, managers get promoted based on their team's performance.**

Strengths and weaknesses of each candidate

Each candidate will have different attributes, experiences, personalities and attitudes. Take the time to make a list of each candidate's strengths and their weaknesses for your position and company. Often seeing this on paper makes a decision much easier.

Would they excel in your position — duplicate their past success?

As we have already stated, the best indicator of future performance is past performance. However, thirty plus years of recruiting has taught me that a high-performer in one position or organization may not be a high-performer in another. You have seen this at your company too. As an example, how many times have we seen a college coach go to the pros and fail miserably? Or a salesperson promoted to a sales manager and flop? So it is important once you identify a high-performer to ask yourself and your hiring committee if the candidate will be able to excel in your company and position as they have done in their past?

So what factors do you look for to make this judgment? Start by asking: Are there different skills/experience /abilities the candidate will need to excel in your company and position?

Take a look at their company. Is the candidate coming from a company that offers support such as manpower or a proven system that the candidate relied on that you cannot offer? I encourage you to think like this. As an example, we have seen employees from large well-run organizations with great systems in place and proven leadership that oversee the employees work. Even an average performer will produce good results in such a system. The system and leadership will ensure that the results are there.

So your task will be to determine the ability of the candidate to reproduce their results with your company and position. This is where intelligent interviewing and reference-checking saves the day.

Look at their current position compared to yours. Some questions to think about may include: Will the candidate be moving up to more responsibilities? If so, intelligent interviewing and good reference-checking will bring clarity here. Let's use a past search for an example to help us.

Case Study: The little engine who could

A long-time client of ours is a large automotive dealership group. They were looking for a service manager and retained us to help conduct the search. We arranged for them to interview 4 or 5 qualified candidates. Several candidates were from equally-sized service departments and one from a much smaller service department. The service manager candidate they liked best was from a smaller service department with 8 automotive technicians and 1 customer service advisor.

Our client's service department had 16 automotive technicians and 3 service advisors. Clearly, we can see that this is a large step up in responsibility for the candidate. The question that needed to be answered was: Can the candidate successfully step up and run a much larger department? To help us evaluate whether the candidate could handle this increased responsibility, we needed to determine their capacity or "ceiling" as we call sometimes call it.

We prepared a list of questions for our client to explore with the candidate. They included questions about managing personnel and what do you do with an underperforming employee. Additionally, we asked a very important question: What do you think will be the difference between your job leading 8 technicians and 1 service advisor and leading our department of 16 technicians and 3 service advisors? Let me tell you, the service manager absolutely nailed this question. From his well-thought-out answer, you could clearly see he thought it through, already had a plan, and extinguished any doubt we had. Not only did he take over this larger staff, by adding several new policies and additional training he grew the department! Without asking real-world, intelligent interviewing questions, our client may have made a different decision.

Had this service manager candidate given us soft answers such as, *Well, I guess people are people* or other sophomoric answers, we would have eliminated him. His answers were well-thought-out and detailed. You could feel his confidence and enthusiasm for the position. In the second interview, he already had a plan in place. He could describe what his introductory meeting would cover and detail his first 30 and 90 days on the job. He communicated how he would evaluate the service department and a timetable on making changes. Without asking the right questions, we would not have the needed information to make an intelligent hiring decision.

Determining capacity is never an exact science. Just look at all the assistant coaches who step up to head coach and fail miserably. To greatly increase your evaluation accuracy, spend time discussing your concerns with the candidate and how they will address them on the job. This will illuminate your understanding of the candidate's ceiling. Using the interviewing questions we described earlier is a great way to learn more about a candidate's abilities. Discussing this with references, especially managers the candidates reported to is also an important part of this equation. Remember our reference checking tip from earlier? Please incorporate it.

Motivation

There is nothing like a highly motivated employee. It is important to determine a candidate's motivation level, but you often have to dig deep to get past the candidate saying all the right things during the interview. I would take a highly motivated candidate with less experience over a poorly motivated but more experienced candidate anytime. Wouldn't you? Would you like to know one of our favorite technique to determine candidate's motivation level? It is a nearly infallible indicator.

One sure sign that you are interviewing a future high performer is ...

Over the past thirty plus years of interviewing candidates and following up on their careers, we have noted one factor that all top-performers share. It is also easy to find out if your candi-

date possesses it — if you know what to look for. If they do possess it, they are very likely to be high-performers for you!

So what is this single magic ingredient that can predict future success? It's been proven to us through thousands of searches that employees who *work hard to develop their professional skills and increase their industry knowledge away from work, at their own expense and time nearly always develop into high-performers in their careers!*

Examples include:

- Sales personnel who practice their presentation at home and record it on their smartphone to review and look for ways to improve.

- Keeping a journal of techniques, ideas, procedures they learned on the job.

- Managers who have put together their own extensive training manual to help them train new employees.

- Reading books on management practices, leadership, customer service, sales, etc., because they want to excel in their job.

- Enrollment in online or weekend classes related to work on their own dime.

- Joining LinkedIn Groups and other online groups and blogs to stay current on their industry.

- Joining clubs like Toastmasters to hone their speaking skills.

What do we ask candidates?

Our wording will vary depending on the level of candidate, but generally here is what we ask:

"What are your career aspirations in the next 5 years?" Listen to their answer then ask:

"What are you doing – away from your workplace — to get to that level?"

After listening to their answer, I may be prompted to ask *"Do you think that is enough to get there?"*

I may be impressed with their answer and more confident that I have a high-performer. If their answer is lacking, I may wonder why they are not putting more effort into developing their skills/knowledge the way high-performers generally do. You may need to prompt them by asking about courses they take, what books they have read the past year to enhance their career, do they have a journal of things they learned in their career, etc?

Case Study: Hiring a sales team for an automotive finance company with a small budget

Throughout my career, I have helped many companies hire sales teams. Many of our clients are in the automotive finance industry. One client, a newly formed automotive finance company, was putting together their very first regional sales team. They retained our services to help them find and select candidates. The issue our client had was that they were new and did not have any name recognition nor deep pockets.

Our client needed to keep fixed expenses low so that they could focus on growth. They could only afford to offer small salaries — much lower than their established competition — but they did offer a larger commission percentage (variable expense). We find this a very common scenario with young growing companies. They also could not afford to offer company cars but would offer a car allowance and have the sales personnel use their own cars.

With a small and very uncompetitive salary, no company car and no name or brand recognition, we knew we would not be able to attract established sales representatives from their competitors. Our client would have to hire people from outside the industry who would see this as a step up in their careers. Established sales representatives saw our client's positions as a step down. It is a mistake to hire someone who sees your position as a step down. Keep in mind, personnel who need a job will take the position even if they see it as a step down, but continue looking and hoping to find a "better position." Don't make this all-too-common hiring mistake.

We explained to our client that their challenge was that they could afford to hire more of a semi-experienced sales representative from outside the industry and that our client would need to train them. We did not want to hire people with zero sales experience. Most people who try sales don't like it. We wanted to have a year or two of sales experience so that the candidate at least knew that they liked sales as a career. You can already see our challenge — how do we determine if these "near-rookie sales people" would excel in our client's positions? As I stated already, the best indicator of future performance is past performance; however these candidates that our client could afford had some, but very little relatable experience.

We used some testing including the DISC test. These are very helpful for learning more about a candidate's inherent abilities, however I'm not Sigmund Freud. These "predictive tests" are in no way a perfect predictor. They are at best helpful. Please note that there is a difference in skills testing such as math skills, keyboarding skills or Excel skills from predictive testing. Skills tests are both accurate and reliable. Predictive tests, where you are trying to predict a candidate's success potential, are much different. Do not make a hiring decision based on a predictive test unless you are working with entry-level positions.

We added to the interview process the question: "Where does the candidate see themselves in 3 to 5 years and what are they doing outside of their workplace to get there?" I was not as interested in where the candidate saw themselves in 3 to 5 years. Candidates will often tell you what they think you want to hear. I am much more interested in what they are doing to get themselves there. This is a very important point. Remember the adage: Actions speak louder than words? I want to know what actions they have undertaken and I want to encourage you to think this way also.

Most candidates we interviewed had very little to give us as far as what they were doing outside of their workplace to help themselves achieve career success. We did not hire them. We focused on hiring candidates who were reading books on sales, subscribed to business magazines, kept journals of techniques they had learned, recorded themselves practicing sales presentations and answering objections.

The search was a great success. With this group of semi-experienced sales personnel, we had about a 75% success rate, which delighted our client and allowed them to gain a firm footing in the automotive finance space. As they grew, they were able to afford to offer more competitive compensation plans and keep their high-performers; several became regional sales managers for our client.

In summary: Employees who put effort into their career improvement - ***on their own time and dime*** - are very likely to be successful with you!

Career seeker Vs. Job seeker

In the recruitment profession, we look for "Career Seekers" over "Job Seekers." There is a world of difference. I teach my recruiters and my clients to look for Career Seekers for several reasons. Career Seekers are looking to "become something more " and "add career value" when they seek a new position. Job Seekers are focused on just getting a job.

Career Seekers will be excited the day they get started because they are beginning a new chapter in their career. The Job Seeker will be happy the ordeal of finding a job is over. Entirely different mindsets! Here are some specifics:

- Career Seekers will likely put more effort into becoming very good and their work.

- Career Seekers will invest more money, effort, and energy in developing their careers.

- Career Seekers are looking long-term and will make decisions that will benefit them long-term.

- Because they are looking long-term, Career Seekers will be more selective and take more time to make a decision. This often frustrates hiring managers.

- Career Seekers will talk to mentors and other trusted people before committing to a new position.

- Job Seekers will come to the interview "all enthused" and will "jump through any hoop" which is attractive to many managers but is not an indicator of high performance. This point is counter-intuitive. To the hiring manager, the Job Seeker looks more attractive during the interview. The Job Seeker is in selling mode and the Career Seeker is in information-gathering mode.

People change positions for a reason. Career Seekers will want to learn about:

- Your position
- The company
- The industry
- You/their mentor

Make it easy for them to learn about these things during the interviewing process.

Two questions that I like to ask that help me learn if I have a Career Seeker or a Job Seeker:

1. Where do you see yourself in 5 years?
2. What are you currently doing to get there?

A Career Seeker will have a plan! The Career Seeker will be enthused when they understand the value your position will add to their career. Keep in mind, companies have many good workers who are not career-oriented. Most of your good, stable workers are not career-oriented. They will show up, do what you ask of them but will not drive themselves or others to achieve beyond what is asked of them.

Do you have the time/capacity/ability to provide adequate training?

When evaluating candidates, it is important to ask yourself and your hiring team what training a new candidate will need and if you have the time and ability to properly train them. Often when evaluating candidates, we need to make this determination. Sometimes companies need to pass on the candidate with that really "high ceiling" and choose a good candidate already trained who is more "plug and play."

I have seen this very early in my headhunting career and you too may need to make these judgment decisions. From time to time, there exists a dilemma: Hire the qualified candidate ready to step in right now, or hire the higher-potential candidates and take time training them?

Case Study: Very busy manager with no time to hire

We have a client who is a large automotive dealership in Chicago. This dealership has a very large and very busy service department. Although this was a large automotive dealership, it was still a small company. Typical for smaller companies, they had no "bench strength." There is no room in their budget to have people on the bench waiting for their turn. Large companies usually have bench strength — personnel being trained and groomed for a role. They are not productive now but will be in the future. Small companies don't think this way. Often, when they lose someone, they have to hire quickly to fill a need. This is when the opportunity for very mediocre or less hires are made.

This service department had customers calling and walking in all day long. It was always busy with service customers waiting in line. When they lost a customer service advisor, it was a disaster. Lines got longer and customer patience was tested. The service manager had to go find an experienced customer service advisor from their competition while doing all the other activities in his already very busy day. Typical of a smaller business, they had no human resources personnel to perform this search.

The service manager had to hire someone quickly because they turn away a lot of service business when they are short-handed, business that may not come back in the future. The service manager made the decision to hire the first experienced customer service advisor who applied. He wanted to plug a leak. This is how mediocre hires are often made. This is the real world. Hire quickly to plug a leak and evaluate on the job. Although I understood the service manager's sense of urgency, I would still recommend spending more time finding and evaluating candidates to make a good hire. This is easy for me to say, but hard for the service manager to actually do in real life when he is responsible for the entire department.

I remember the service manager telling me that he had to get someone ASAP. With the owner and general manager checking his department's numbers every day, the manufacturer checking by the hour, a line of customers in front of him and 25 other personnel to manage, he spent all the time he could on the search. As he said, "I have more pressing issues to deal with." You too may face this situation. How would you handle it? How would you want your subordinates to handle it? These are the real-world decisions managers at small companies make all the time.

Cultural fit

Wikipedia states **organizational culture** encompasses values and behaviors that "contribute to the unique social and psychological environment" of an organization. In my years of professional recruitment, I have learned how important corporate culture can be to one's success at a company.

Early in my career we performed many searches looking for personnel for subprime automotive finance companies. We learned that bankers – who have the same job responsibilities such as credit underwriting, collections, sales – are a terrible cultural fit for subprime automotive finance companies. They perform the same work but the difference in cultures made it very difficult to adapt from one to the other.

I remember one banker who moved to a subprime automotive finance company. He called me and communicated that he left his bank about 6 months earlier to join a rapidly growing subprime automotive finance company as their director of credit. I remember him asking me if I can help get him a position with another bank. He explained to me that the subprime automotive finance company was loosely managed, with few rules, and most of the people he was dealing with did not have college degrees. Worst of all was that the clientele the company was chasing were the exact clientele his bank avoided! He was a terrific director of credit for a stable bank, but he was a fish out of water for a rapidly growing subprime finance company.

The lesson I learned here is that you must explain your corporate culture to the candidates. Let them meet with and talk to your employees and the candidates will better understand the cultural differences. Discuss this with the candidates and see how they feel about the differences. The majority of times, corporate cultures are similar enough that it won't make a big difference. However in some situations it can be a deal-breaker.

Knockout factors

Save time, aggravation and professional embarrassment!

We have learned the value of establishing *"**Knockout Factors**"* at the beginning of every search. These are factors that are so important that, no matter how qualified a candidate may otherwise be, they will be "knocked out of contention" by one factor.

You may have been there yourself. A typical example is hiring a sales representative, letter of intent already presented contingent upon background check. Background checks come back and reveal that your #1 candidate has too many points on their driver's license to be insured with your company. No matter how qualified – game over!

Worse, I know a large company that was about to hire a CFO. After two months of interviewing, committee meetings about the candidate, interviews with members of the BOD and key investors and letter of intent sent, contingent upon background check, a problem arose — they found that the CFO had a non-compete that he could not get out of. Game over, lots of professional embarrassment. The CEO was livid – careers changed that day for allowing that mistake.

To spare our clients from these issues, we prepare a list of "knockout factors" when beginning a search such as:

- Candidate's ability to commute to your office daily or relocate. Spouses play a crucial role in relocation, so make sure spouse's input is received early in the process.

- Does a non-compete exist?

- Has specific knowledge necessary such as "Excel Expertise?"

- Needed licensure (driver's license needed to do job or CPA required, etc.)?

- Credit and criminal background checks needed?

- Ability to travel as required.

- Bad attitude?

These issues are easy to resolve up front.

- If a candidate has concerns about **location of office**, we have them make the drive in rush hour traffic to see if it is a reasonable drive day to day. Don't forget to factor in winter driving here up north.

- We ask about **non-compete** up front. If there is one, we want to see it. We let our client know about it and they can determine how it may affect them. Some are limited to industry, geographic area, prime vs subprime financing, etc. Many are game-ending.

- We ask about **ability to travel**. Generally we do not consider candidates for a travel position, (such as a regional sales manager), if they are not in a travel position. Travel sounds glamorous, but it is a grind. Most people cannot do it.

- When it comes to **credit, background and driver license** checks, we tell candidates about these requirements up front. Should the candidate have an issue, they will either take themselves out of the process or tell us about their situation to see if it is workable. If they know about these requirements and try to keep them from us – they are immediately disqualified.

- If I may share a 30-plus-years-of-recruitment experience with you: As soon as a candidate's "**bad attitude**" is revealed, end any and all thoughts of hiring the candidate. Bad attitudes are contagious and no amount of technical skill will overcome the issues they can cause on your team!

Make a list of "knockout factors" before you start any search; it will save you time, aggravation, and professional embarrassment.

'CEILING' VS. 'GETTING THEM UP TO SPEED'

In the executive search profession, we are always comparing candidates as we decide who "makes the cut" and gets sent to our client and who does not. We look at many factors in making our decisions, but I want to talk about two factors that will bring clarity to your group of candidates fairly quickly. This is the candidate's ceiling versus what it takes to get them up to speed.

We look at the potential "ceiling " a candidate may have. This is how high do we think this candidate can rise? This is easier for a candidate whose performance can be measured: sales, sales management, department head; CEOs are good examples where their performance is fairly easy to measure.

You can also use this concept when looking at positions that may not have such measurables. Example: You are looking at accounting manager candidates. After interviewing the candidates, you begin the final selection process. Who in the group looks like they have the "higher ceiling?" That is, who may have the ability to become a divisional manager? Corporate controller? CFO?

As an example, let's assume you are looking at your group of good accounting manager candidates: all have degrees, good work experience, good references, and interviewed well. The candidates with the "higher ceiling" may be more attractive to your company.

In a recent search we completed for a CEO for a mid-size automotive company, we had several very impressive candidates that ownership and the search committee liked. They debated candidates for several days, then in a conference call they asked me what I thought. I told them I will ask one question and I think your answer will emerge immediately after. They were intrigued.

I communicated that the finalists are all very good candidates with terrific experiences, accomplishments, etc. Now, which candidate has the highest ceiling? All agreed on one candidate right away! Conversation then moved to putting an offer together.

There is a balance to "highest ceiling" that needs to be factored in and that is what will it take to get this candidate up to speed for your open position? As an example, let's assume you are looking for a regional manager for a 12-person department. Good-sized responsibility.

The candidates with the highest ceiling may look like they possess the potential to really grow your department someday and possibly branch you into other industries, but may lack needed experience for the fast-paced department they need to head now. The job at hand is regional manager and you may need a "plug and play" leader ready to go now — ***you cannot look past this fact***! What will it take to get the best candidate "up to speed for your position?" So discuss with your hiring committee:

- What is the cost and time required to get this candidate trained and "up to speed?"

- Can you afford a period of time for this candidate to develop:

  > Product knowledge?

  > More knowledge about your industry? Your customers?

  > Fluency with your corporate technology?

- Is this a much larger staff than they have ever managed?

Very often companies need to pass on the candidate with the highest ceiling and focus on the candidate that can do the very best with the position they are hiring for now. This is more typical with smaller companies. Remember our earlier discussion regarding the automotive service manager hiring a customer service advisor? Larger companies often have bench strength. They have time to develop staff. Smaller companies almost never have bench strength. Managers with smaller companies have no luxury of time nor bench strength and often make the decision to hire a plug and play individual even if they are mediocre.

This is the" Ceiling vs Getting them up to speed" decision you sometimes need to make.

TAKE AWAY: Go into each interview looking for clues to a candidate's "potential ceiling" and what will be needed to get the candidate "up to speed" for your open position.

DECIPHERING A CANDIDATE'S EMPLOYMENT RECORD DURING THE INTERVIEW - MADE EASY

The best indicator of a candidate's future performance with you is their past performance. But you have to know what to look for!!!

Employment behavior tends to follow consistent patterns. A low-achiever has a record of low achievement and a high-achiever has a record of high achievement. The confusing part is deciphering a candidate's employment record during the interview and evaluation process.

Low-achievers are usually very good at "hiding" in successful departments. As an interviewer, it is your responsibility to find out the actual contributions, accomplishments, and employment record of the candidate to determine if a high- or low-achiever is sitting in front of you. In 30 years of recruiting, we have learned that one of the most common mistakes employers make is hiring low-performers from successful companies.

As the interviewer, you must ask the questions that will yield the information you need to make a smart hiring decision.

During the interview, probe candidates about their accomplishments, their specific role, dates and time frames, awards, bonuses, promotions, attendance, and good teammate traits.

Then verify with references. Do not miss the "verify with references " part. Learn from the finance and banking industry – they do not just ask customers "how they pay their bills" do they? No, they verify – so should you!

Don't allow important questions to be answered with soft answers. They provide you with no real assessment value. Ask for facts, details and information to support their contributions and references who will verify them.

Revealing questions

In 30 years of recruitment, we have found certain questions can be very revealing. Of course, many questions will be asked, but keep the 80/20 rule in mind when it comes to revealing questions. The following is an example that I use when interviewing sales managers. Whether your position is a group VP over multiple locations or a sales manager for a small staff, a few intelligent questions reveal so much from the interview.

Now watch as I drill down for specifics and remember that the devil lies in the detail.

EXAMPLE – Sales Manager:

After a general discussion about our client's sales staff and its strengths and weaknesses, **I ask**: *Now that you know the issues our client has with its sales staff, tell me how you will help their sales staff perform much better for you than they are now.*

Candidate answer: *I will motivate them to sell.*

My follow up: *Walk me through the details of how you have done that in the past.*

Candidate answer: *I will train them to be better; I'm a great trainer.*

My follow up: *Share some significant details about your training program and walk me through your "From-To" results.*

Candidate answer: *I will hold them accountable for their results.*

My follow up: *That sounds great, let's talk about your current system to hold your people accountable...*

I do not allow for soft or generic answers to specific questions. You shouldn't either. The high-performers will have specific answers and be able to support their "From-To" results.

You as the interviewer must lead and ask the questions that will yield the information you need to make a smart hiring decision. Become great at developing these revealing questions and pursuing details so that you can decipher a candidate's true employment record.

Please keep in mind we are not trying to stump a candidate; we want to learn about them so we can make an astute judgment on how they will perform in the future with our client.

UNDERSTANDING 'KNOWLEDGE VS DRIVE' AND WHY IT MATTERS

You've been there, every hiring manager has. You interview a person who "aced the interview," "blows you away," and asks, no demands, the job during the interview! You hire that candidate with great anticipation only to be surprised to see them fizzle after a few months instead of providing the sizzle you expected.

Why so much anticipation and so little production?

Knowledge vs Drive

People from your industry come to the interview with a lot of knowledge. They have heard the wisdom of very good managers and know how to offer that knowledge up during an interview as if it is their way of doing business. They know the questions to ask to get you excited.

Example: Experienced sales representative interviewing with an automotive dealership:

They may ask a question like: *"If I am fortunate enough to receive this position, would it be OK to call all my friends and relatives, I come from a big family? I really want to hit the ground running! Can I do that?"* And drool rolls out of the sales manager's mouth hearing this!

Example: Manager candidate:

They may recite during the interview words that they were taught (whether they practice these is an entirely different issue), such as: *"Let me tell you about my leadership style. I believe in leading from the front, I like to be visible to the team. I like to jump in on their harder deals. After all, it is a lot easier to pull a piece of string from the front than push from the back, isn't it?"* Now the hiring manager of the company is swiveling around in their chair, so happy to have found this candidate.

The question is can these candidates' interview performances live up to their work performance? The answer is that it will depend on their "Drive." They have the knowledge of business and position, and they know what they should be doing, but do they have the drive to do this? If they do, it will be shown in their performance and work results. You need to take the time to find this out.

For now, I want you to be thinking — does the candidate possess the drive to accompany their knowledge to perform at a high level day-to-day, bell-to-bell, month-after-month? Or will they "suck it up for the interview" and talk the talk and not walk the walk?

Going to our sales representative example: If they have been in the business for just one year, they have a lot of knowledge of the business and what it takes to succeed. They know the basics and what is needed to excel and serve it up during the interview. They also have heard many great sales tips that they like to share during the interview.

The knowledge is there – but you need to look for drive. We have learned over the years that human nature follows a pattern and does not change much in our prime working years. So we look for the patterns that produce success. People need a lot of "drive" to be successful. So look for these patterns. Ask the salesperson how many times in the last 12 months they hit quota. Can they lie to us? Sure can! So we always ask to "show me" sales records, or paychecks to see if they are hitting their bonuses every month as they say they are. Did they get nominated for sales representative of the month? Year? Can they provide corroborating references, etc.? We have learned that top-performers will bring their accomplishments to an interview and low-achievers will bring excuses and stories. We have learned to be wary of candidates with stories when they are not achieving at higher levels. **Show me the money!**

Candidate Stories

How many times have you bought into candidate stories? This was my hiring weakness early in my career. I often made the mistake of hiring personnel who were just "looking for the right opportunity." I bought into their frustration for not being successful in their careers and their desire to achieve. I saw myself there early in my career, looking for that first opportunity out of college. My belief was that I was a terrific trainer and I would provide the training, coaching, and the environment for them to excel. I mistakenly bought into their stories that this was what had been lacking in their careers to date.

I was too naive back then to understand that these people were just serial low-performers who knew how to tell stories absolving themselves of their own career shortcomings. Once hired, their flaws would show themselves quickly. Typically, they came in unprepared, did not study materials I gave to them and were missing work. Often I followed up by trying to motivate them, champion their cause and prod them to achieve as we had discussed in their interviews.

The problem was that I wanted them to succeed more than they did. Have you made this mistake early in your hiring career? I bet you have. I did not have a mentor to tell me what mistake I was making by empathizing with them instead of performing my job of scrutinizing and assessing them to ensure that I was making the best hires for my company. Do you have someone on your staff who is making this common hiring mistake? If you do, discuss this issue with them. Make them aware of their assessment shortcoming.

Later in my career, I found a mentor, a client who was a very seasoned and very wealthy entrepreneur. He made a fortune in real estate development, retired in his 50s. Then he started another company renting automobiles to people whose cars were in repair shops. He took this company public and took a spin off of it public also. This was a man from a very humble background who made several fortunes in his life. Like most of these very successful individuals, he liked to help people who are looking to move up. He was in his 70s when I met him and I talked with him often as his new company was growing rapidly. After each meeting with him, usually to fill an executive opening, I would ask him for a business lesson. He would always look at me, smile and share career-changing wisdom.

One terrific lesson he taught me that I want to share with you is about dealing with underperforming employees. He taught me that as soon as he sees an employee is not capable or simply unwilling to do the job required, he makes a change. If the employee is a good employee — good attitude, on time, works hard — he will reassign them into a position that may be a better fit for them. He would give a good employee several chances to find their niche with him. He did not hold it against them if they performed subpar in one position as long as they perform well in the reassigned position.

If he thought that the employee was simply unwilling to put in the effort to succeed, he would fire that person quickly. He explained that, by getting rid of an employee who is performing on a subpar level due to lack of effort, poor attitude, etc., he was doing a number of people a favor, including the terminated employee. How is that, I inquired? He explained that the employee who is unwilling to put forth the effort is probably feeling under a lot of stress, and if this person has a family the stress is likely affecting the family. Let this person be freed up to seek a better position for themselves where they will perform better and be happier.

He further explained that the employee's subpar performance is likely negatively affecting their co-workers too. If the person is a manager and performing subpar, they will definitely be affecting a team of employees and putting stress on them. If the team is then performing subpar, that will negatively affect other groups they associate with in the company and possibly with our customers and suppliers. After listening to him, I realized that he was not callous at all. He really had everyone's best interest in mind including the person being terminated.

Getting back to recognizing our Knowledge vs Drive discussion, high-performers can prove their performance, if asked. Often you do not even have to ask; they will bring proof during the 1st interview or even include evidence along with their resume.

For High-performers — Knowledge will be on par with their performance.

For Low-performers — Knowledge will exceed their performance.

When you are interviewing, keep in mind Knowledge vs Drive and how to determine this!

High Performer

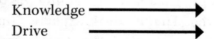

Low Performer

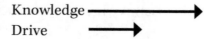

PRACTITIONER VS THEORIST AND HOW TO TELL THE DIFFERENCE

You have been here many times. You interview several candidates and each sounds terrific. Your senses tell you that not all would thrive in your position, but you are confused as to who would and who would not thrive.

Allow me to share a recruiting secret that has helped our firm successfully place several thousand candidates with our clients over the past 30 years. It is a simple mental paradigm that helps us weed through a group of great-sounding candidates and get to the winning hires for our clients.

When several candidates interview well and sound great, try asking yourself and your hiring team if you are working with one: **"Who are the Practitioners and who are the Theorists?"** Theorists can certainly talk the talk, but Practitioners walk the walk. Which do you need?

Characteristics of Theorists:

- Openly very knowledgeable – you likely won't need to prompt them for information.

- Quick on their feet, verbally intelligent. Sound very smart (and usually are).

- In charge of facts and statistics.

- Probably enjoys the interview process and talking shop.

- Superficial on details of their specific role and what they accomplished.

- They know how to tell you "what you want to hear."

- References are usually co-workers not their direct managers.

Characteristics of the Practitioner:

- Very knowledgeable – however you may need to prompt them during the interview for information.

- Sound smart and are smart.

- Can talk easily about challenges, how they overcame them and results. May or may not have statistics committed to memory.

- May not enjoy the interviewing process and talking shop, unless they are talking to a peer with a similar background. They like doing the work. They tolerate human resources questions but do not like them.

- Can be very precise on their specific role in what they accomplished.

- They will tell you how things really are.

- References are usually their past managers and bosses.

Why might this shed light on your hiring process?

The **Theorists** can *talk the talk* – and talk it very well, but may come up short on *walking the walk*. The **Practitioner** may come up a little short on *talking the talk* (without some prompting), but will *walk the walk* for you. This is why knowing what to look for is so important!

Here is our formula

- It is very important to learn and talk about their specific accomplishments.

- Drill down on the specifics such as productivity went from **X to X+**. Ask for some verification. Talk is cheap, facts are not!

- Drill down on their specific role.

- Ask about what issues they ran into.

- Ask how they overcame the issues.

- Ask for specifics, engage in a discussion of details.

- Spend time with references learning about the candidate's actual accomplishments and whether it matches the candidate's claims.

Theorists are often "corporate survivors," not the true "organizational drivers." They have hung around for years and learned a lot. They are great at articulating facts, but lack the ability to make the crucial decisions that lead to success. Usually they lack leadership skills and often try to avoid having to make important decisions. They are very tuned into corporate politics.

Practitioners are the "organizational drivers." They are the employees who get things done. They take action. In football analogy, think of Bill Belichick as a role model for Practitioner and think of a TV football analyst or sports writer as a role model Theorist. I would hire Bill Belichick to run my team even though Peter King of *Sports Illustrated* may do a better job of articulating a team's history.

Take Away: Hire the Practitioner because they have made the successful decisions, built the well-run departments, and can tell you how if you know how to ask them.

FOUR TYPES OF PERSONALITIES - AND HOW TO WIN WITH EACH, OR AT LEAST NOT LOSE!

Psychologists study many aspects of human personality. Here is a simple way to look at four personality types you will encounter during interviews, with current employees, customers, vendors, and anyone else you will meet. Knowing the type of person you are dealing with often helps you understand them better and brings some clarity as to how to deal with them. I am sure you have heard of each of these four personality types before; however, I want to discuss them here for you to keep in mind when interviewing and assessing candidates. Certain personality types are great fits for some positions and disasters for others.

Another mistake that I made early in my career of hiring people is thinking that if someone is intelligent, they can perform well in nearly any role or assignment you give them. I thought that, if they had strong mental capacity, they could both learn and perform well in most any role. Huge mistake!

A person's personality has a great effect on their capacity to perform a job. Early on in my career, I did not know that being able to learn a job and the ability to perform it well day to day are two separate things. Performing well means more than just being able to learn what to do. Let's take a look at the four personality types and think about how they may perform in a position with you.

1. **Passive**

   Key trait is difficulty speaking up, fear of conflict, frequently apologizing, and often when it is not necessary.

   You may need to: empower them to communicate and provide a psychological safety net for them to do their best work. Catch them doing things right.

   Best Position: Usually they are uncomfortable making judgment decisions. Better for repetitive roles where they can learn the job and perform it well day-to-day, such as clerical roles.

2. **Aggressive**

   Key trait is an instinctive response to argue, feel threatened, resist new information, and difficulty controlling their emotions.

   You may need to: let them know that you are listening, such as "If I understand what you are saying is ...." Repeating it back to them often calms the Aggressive type down because they understand that you are listening to them.

Best Position: They can become terrific sales personnel but the Aggressive type can also be a disaster dealing with customers if they cannot control their emotions. Their tendency is to argue instead of applying persuasion. Your hope is that they will evolve into Assertive behavior from Aggressive. Aggressive personalities can cause conflict with co-workers and cause rancor among the troops. I have a belief, no data to support this, however: I think that Aggressive personalities may lead to more lawsuits than all the other personality types together. Be wary of the Aggressive personality type.

3. **Passive–Aggressive**

   Key trait is being polite to your face while planning to stab you in the back or otherwise hurt you. They often control their emotions in-front of you then act out later. This is the person who will key your car to "get back at you" instead of discussing a problem.

   You may need to: keep an eye on this type if you have to deal with them. They often try to "control what others' think about you."

   Best Position: Is working for someone else, hopefully your competitor!

4. **Assertive**

   Key trait is they will speak their mind and control their emotions. You can have frank and productive conversations with the Assertive personality.

   You may need to: Be prepared for them to ask for something for their benefit in any communication.

Best Position: Most good sales representatives, managers and executives are Assertive types. If you think about why, they need to get things done through other people, motivate others, and turn "no" into "yes."

I hope this helps add perspective to your personnel searches, candidate assessments, and in your daily interactions. Think about the position you are filling. Will they need to perform the same routine over and over, or will they need to make deep assessments and judgment decisions? Will they need to motivate the troops, sell a product in a competitive marketplace? The lesson I had to learn is that their personality type will have a tremendous influence on their ability to perform in your position.

CANDIDATE MINDSET: DO YOU NEED A STEADY EDDIE, STAR, OR A HERO?

I learned a technique many years ago that has been very helpful. Fortunately, I learned this technique early in my career. I want to share it with you. This is another way to look at any position you are filling. It takes into account the candidate's mindset. You want to know more than whether the candidate has performed well in the same role at another company. Mindset is about fit. This concept is best illustrated by example.

As an example, let's say you are looking for someone to replace a retiring person and take over a well-run department with no changes needed. You want that "Steady Eddie" mindset who will do just that. Take over, get everything done, and make few if any changes and keep employees happy.

If you need someone to come in and "raise the bar," you need that "Star" mindset. This person will come in and work crazy hours and make all the changes needed to improve performance. They will rankle some existing personnel who are underperforming while driving the staff to higher levels. You may lose some employees if you hire a Star, however the Star will endeavor to improve results.

From time to time, our clients are looking for someone to fix a mess, perhaps a department, a division, or an entire company. For this we are looking for the "Hero." The person who will cut, slash, redistribute and make many changes to totally reorganize and re-energize. Lee Iacocca did this for Chrysler in the 1980s and Alan Mulally for Ford. Heroes will often be disliked by some of the current staff but loved by others who want to see the problems fixed.

The person looking for a Steady Eddie job will be a disaster if a Star or Hero is needed. If a Steady Eddie mindset is needed to take over an existing well-run position, then putting a Hero in place will also be a mess. This Hero will try to shake things up that may not need to be shaken up and soon leave for more challenging opportunities. Often after they have messed up an entire staff.

How many times have you made this mistake, hiring a person with the right experience but wrong mindset? What I want you to know about this mindset concept is it will not show up in a resume. It is in a person's head. So ask yourself, what do you need: a Steady Eddie to keep things the same, a Star to raise the bar, or a Hero to make wholesale changes? Don't get this wrong; it is important. Discuss this during your interviewing and assessment process.

At our firm, we incorporate this language in our job postings and in our presentation to potential candidates that we contact. Let's look at 3 sub-headlines for examples:

"Hero needed to restructure ......"

"Star needed to raise the bar......"

"Stable company needs to replace retiring ...."

See how this language will attract the candidates with the right mindset?

Here is what I want you to think about while applying this concept. Add this dimension to your search when you are hiring anyone overseeing other employees. From a supervisor of four people to a CEO for an entire company. When you begin your search, think about the position and what needs to be accomplished beyond duties and responsibilities. Think in terms of changes that may or not be needed.

When you are interviewing candidates, share this with them. Some candidates will pass on a position because you need to make few changes because it is an already well-run department, and that Star or Hero will be under-challenged and not interested in your position. Should they accept your position, they will soon be unhappy and leave for a greater challenge because their mindset is not in line with the needs of the position.

If you need to "raise the bar" or make large changes and you hire that Steady Eddie type, they will be over-stressed and unhappy with the position. Their mindset is just not up to the task at hand. They may tough it out and get it done, however they also may not. You will be much better off hiring a candidate with the right mindset. I want you to think like this and avoid this very common hiring mistake.

Mindsets can and do change over time during one's career. What we have often seen is a successful young person may possess that Star mindset. They are at a point early in their career where they can take risk. Roll the dice and go with a young startup company. Perhaps they are keen to open a new division with a large established company. They are excited to put themselves in a fast-paced position where they are working constantly, achieving and growing. They can afford to take a risk at this point and will be OK if the startup suddenly goes under. When you talk to a Star mindset, they will light up when you contact them about a startup company with large ambitions. They will be nonplussed if you contact them to discuss a stable company not growing.

We also see candidates further along in their careers who want to avoid risk and the long hours. How many times have we heard very successful mid-career candidates tell us that: "I have 3 kids that I will be putting through college while paying a large mortgage over the next 10 years." " I am looking for a solid, stable company in a stable industry." Of course this person is. They cannot afford any income disruption for the next 8 to 10 years. That is what is controlling the mindset of a Steady-Eddie. It may have turned a Star mindset into a Steady Eddie mindset. This Steady Eddie mindset employee will work very hard and endeavor to be a model employee. Talk to this person about joining a startup company and they may cringe.

Now the young Star mindset who turned into a Steady-Eddie while raising a family calls us after the children are all graduated from college, tuitions and mortgage paid off. What might they tell us they are looking for? Frequently they want something more exciting in their career again. They are now in a position to once again take a chance. Perhaps go with a startup or become a Hero and use their decades of experience and wisdom and turn around a mess. Often they want to relocate to a more exciting city. See how mindset can change during one's career?

Case Study: Terrible-sounding job just needed a Hero

As I stated earlier, I am fortunate to have learned this very valuable concept early on. It has helped my recruitment firm eliminate hundreds of hiring mistakes while interviewing terrific employees who did not have the correct mindset. An early search in my career was for an automotive dealership in my hometown of Cleveland, Ohio. I can still remember the stress in the voice of the automotive dealership owner when he called me.

His controller had just left and gave no notice. This alone put him in a lurch because there was no one at the dealership to step into the role. Small companies do not have bench strength. However, there was a much larger problem. The controller left the dealership in a terrible mess. The dealer told me that there was an entire room of unreconciled checks dating back years. Their warranty paperwork was way off and way behind. Warranty work is very important to an automotive dealership because they earn a lot of their revenue from the manufacturer compensating for the warranty work they perform in their service department. They were hundreds of thousands of dollars upside down with a time limit on when they can submit warranty work and still be paid for it.

The dealer had focused on the sales aspect for the dealership and trusted in the controller to do her part, which she had not. The dealer explained that he and his wife were in the office all weekend just trying to get their arms around the mess. This was a huge mess, the dealer did not know his true cash position and knew that he was losing dollars every day by not collecting on the warranty work correctly.

The dealer was beside himself. I remember his voice tremble when he said that his wife asked him who would ever want to come in and fix this mess? The dealer explained that it will take a pro a year to 18 months to resolve this and they will need to work 7 days a week in the beginning just to stem the hemorrhaging. I knew just what to do. I knew they needed a Hero. I also knew just what to tell local automotive dealership controllers when we contacted them.

I had recently hired a new recruiter and brought him in to assist with the search. I explained to him that we needed a Hero. This would be a good lesson for him too. I knew that when he contacted local controllers and explained the huge problem that needed to be turned around that nearly everyone would say "no way do I want to take on that mess." He asked a question that I anticipated him asking: "Then we shouldn't tell them what a huge mess it is upfront?" My answer was not at all what he expected. What this young recruiter did not yet understand is that the mess that needed to be fixed was the selling point!

I told him cleaning up this huge mess is the selling point! We will get many answers of "no" until we come across that Hero looking for more challenge. He and I both started calling local automotive dealership controllers. As expected, they could not say no fast enough. When we asked if they were not interested could they recommend someone they knew, their answers were often "I wouldn't wish this mess upon anyone."

Then one call hit pay dirt. One controller we talked to was excited that there was such a challenge out there! She had a great job as a controller, however she was bored. She had already groomed a bookkeeper to do much of her controllership work and made her assistant office manager. We arranged for this controller to meet the dealer and his wife on Saturday morning. They spent the day together going through the mess and she already started to organize things and put them in perspective. She informed them that they lost several hundred thousand dollars in warranty work not submitted, but their cash position was manageable.

They offered her the job that day; she accepted. She arranged with her current dealer a workout period to change all duties over to her assistant office manager to become the-full-time office manager. Additionally, she would start working nights and weekends at the new dealership getting them back up to speed. I remember the happiness in her voice when she called me that Saturday after she met with the dealer and his wife telling me that she had accepted the job! I remember her telling me that the dealer and his wife think it will take a year to 18 months but I will have this office spinning like a top in 6 months. And she did! The lesson I wanted this young recruiter to learn is that this wasn't a terrible job. It was a great job, for a Hero!

I want you to think about this too. Let's imagine that a controller had been moving into the area and was desperate for a job, but was not a Hero personality. Had they come across the position, they may have taken it. However, they likely would have failed at it and left. Remember that a resume does not tell you anything about a candidate's mindset. You need to explore it with the candidate. Watch their reaction and then make a judgment decision whether or not the candidate possesses the right mindset for the position.

The Great Question we discussed earlier will help you with this. When we ask our clients — **A year from now, what will the candidate need to accomplish to be considered a terrific hire?** This helps us get to mindset. It illuminates improvements that the new hire will be responsible for. I want you to think like this too. Using this technique will help you avoid this common hiring mistake as it has helped our firm for the past 30 years.

CHAPTER 6

OFFER AND NEGOTIATIONS

WE HAVE A rule in our office – never make an offer unless you know it will be accepted. So how do we know if an offer will be accepted? During the interviewing process, we seed questions in that will test what a candidate is thinking. In sales, these are called "trial closes." These questions can often influence a candidate's thinking.

Here is an example during the interview process:

You are interviewing candidates for a position and during the interviews you tell each candidate: " *The candidates we are* *interviewing are in the $95,000 to $110,000 range. Does that meet your expectations?"*

If the candidate say no, then ask them where they need to be. At this point, you are finding out what an offer needs to be for the candidate without making a commitment.

Same if the candidate's answer is yes. We now know their range. We test this range several times during the interview process. Remember, take your time interviewing and have several interviews.

So why does this question work so well? It is all about perceived competition. If a candidate wants your position and feels that there is competition for it, they are usually willing to take less so that they don't price themselves out of the picture. The reverse is also true. If the candidate feels that they are the top candidate, or worse for you, feels that they are your only candidate, they will leverage this and ask for more money – wouldn't you?

Test again in later interviews:

> *We are looking at several very good candidates. Here is the offer we are thinking is fair. _____What's your thinking?*

Again, we are using the benefit of perceived competition to our advantage with this question. Additionally, we are not locking ourselves into an offer or a hard number yet.

We use this same question prior to making an offer. This is an important step and I want to teach it to you.

THE FINAL 'TEST CALL'

We like to call the chosen candidate but not yet tell them they are the chosen candidate. We test the offer and keep their thinking from spinning out of control. It is easy to do if you know how and will make it so much easier to call a great candidate. The call looks like this:

"We plan to have a decision by Thursday. Did anything change on your end?"

"OK, still interested?"

"Great, the offer we are thinking here is:

- Title of position is _____
- Start date of _____
- Base salary of _____
- Bonus of _____
- 3 weeks' vacation starting _____
- Other _____

"If we offer you the position, is all that acceptable to you?"

Does this look a little like closing a car sale? "$3,000 down $5,000 for your trade-in and $500 per month."

Yes, this is classic deal closing. Testing the offer before it is made. It is more frictionless when you approach a candidate this way.

If the candidate wants the position, they may be more flexible when they feel there is competition. If there is an issue, such as more money, we can ask what they are looking for without committing. Negotiating money can often upset people. You are telling them in a sense what you think they are worth. This is a much gentler way of negotiating money because it is still a hypothetical. This is a very important point about this technique and why it makes closing much more friendly.

It should be expected that a candidate will ask for more of something with base salary being the most common. Expect this and be prepared for it.

Candidates frequently say something such as: *"Well I was looking for a base salary of $10,000 more than that."*

We then respond with: *"Is that a deal-breaker?"*

Let's say their answer is yes that's a deal-breaker.

I would respond with: *"Tell me more about what you are thinking?"*

Candidate say: "I was thinking $10,000 more in base salary is a minimum. And I will deliver that back to you in job performance."

Possible response from you is: *Is there a figure in-between that may satisfy you and stay nearer to our parameters?"*

Remember you have maximum leverage at this point. If their answer is: *"Yes, I will meet you halfway"* then you just saved $5,000.

If their answer is: *"No I need to be $10,000 above your base salary,"* then you know where your offer needs to be if you want to hire that candidate. After discussing the point, I will ask if we can meet your salary demands, do we have an agreement on the other points. This is a staple of negotiating: If I can meet your demand on this point, do we have a deal?

The candidate may want to change several other items too. Your job here is to see what it will take to get a firm commitment from the candidate. The more "trial closes" you incorporate during the interviewing process, the less candidate push back you will get at the close.

Remember, discussing money at this point is a much softer approach and is less likely to upset a good candidate if your offer is too low.

Candidate's request are inversely proportional to their interest.

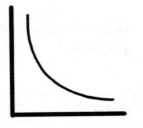

Inverse Proportion

The more a candidate wants a position is inversely proportional to what they ask for.

The more they want the position the less they will ask for. The less they want the position, the more they will ask for to make a move.

We gauge a candidate's interest level by how much they ask for. The more they want, the less interested they are. Asking for too much is a good sign that the candidate is not very interested and will likely shop your offer to their current company hoping for a raise. We walk away from greedy candidates.

Outside factors can impact your candidate's thinking

A good example is when a candidate is looking at other positions congruent with yours. If they are smart, they will leverage this potential competition. For instance, when testing your candidate with:

We are looking at several very good candidates. Here is the offer we are thinking is fair. _____What's your thinking?

The candidate may respond with: "The other positions I am considering are $15,000 to $20,000 above that," and watch how you respond.

Smart candidate's often say this whether it is true or not. Part of smart negotiating is creating competition. Now you have a decision to make.

Keep in mind, a hot candidate will have other offers and they may be more than you are planning on or willing to pay. Remember this, the market sets the price for great candidates — you do not. Smart candidates will know what they are worth and will hold out for it.

NEGOTIATION TOLERANCE

The more sophisticated a position and candidate, the more tolerance the candidate will have for negotiations. When we fill C-Level roles for larger corporations, the negotiations can go on for weeks. That's with both sides working hard and being flexible. But for many positions, the candidate will get turned off if they have to negotiate and are prone to pulling out.

Office staff, technical, and lower-level personnel will not negotiate very much before they become frustrated and look elsewhere. They will tell you, if asked, what they are looking for in the first interview. If you won't pay that, then they are usually more inclined to look at other companies than negotiate with you. Office staff frequently get intimidated if they have to start negotiating and will pull out and look elsewhere. In these types of positions, the candidate will usually want to interview only once, maybe twice.

Executives are a different breed. They will often want to meet with ownership or senior management several times over a period of several weeks along with the management staff. They will want time to review financials, establish expectations, and agree on responsibilities. They are very inclined to negotiate and play hardball and enjoy the process.

Keep the concept of negotiation tolerance in mind when interviewing.

Offer in Person or by Phone?

Each can be effective. Since we work with companies around the United States, almost all of our offers are presented over the phone. When I started my career, I worked with companies around Cleveland, Ohio and made many offers in person for our clients. Some clients like to make the offer themselves. Most that do still like to present the offer on the phone. From my experience, each method is effective if you have a motivated candidate and a good offer.

Here is what we have learned to do to make the offer go well. First, we should know what the candidate will accept from our "test offers" during the interview.

This should be done before you make the offer.

"We plan to have a decision by Thursday. Did anything change on your end?"

"OK, still interested?"

"Great, the offer we are thinking here is:

- Title of position is _____
- Start date of _____
- Base salary of _____
- Bonus of _____
- 3 weeks vacation starting_____
- Other." _____

All points are agreed to or changes that candidate needs to see are worked out and understood.

In person

When possible, I like to have the candidate come in and make the offer in person. A letter of intent covering all points can be delivered to the candidate and have them sign there or take home and review and bring back when starting. If all is good, you shake hands and everyone is happy. If there needs to be some massaging of the offer, you can usually talk through it while the candidate is there.

By phone

Making an offer via phone is pretty much the same. We make the great majority of our offers over the phone. Let them know you are happy to have them join your team. Make the offer, massage fine points if needed, and let them know you will send a letter of intent covering all points for them to review, sign, and return a copy.

Many hiring managers are more comfortable calling the candidate and telling them that they are offering them the position and will send (usually via email) a letter of intent covering all points. Once the candidate receives the letter, they can call if they have any questions. Otherwise they are requested to sign and return a copy of the signed letter to the company or bring it with them on their first day of work.

If you have the right candidate and a fair offer, either method works.

PRESENTING A PAY PLAN THAT WILL BE ACCEPTED

Here is what we learned about presenting a pay plan.

By the time you get to offering the position to a candidate, you should know what it will take to get the candidate on board.

Trial Closes: During the interview process we test trial closes to gauge a candidate's needs, such as: "We are interviewing several good sales manager candidates and the pay range they are looking for is around $150K all in with a base salary of $85K. How does that align with your needs?"

If we are way off, let's find out now. Perhaps you cannot afford this candidate or maybe you need to find a way to stretch your budget to bring them aboard.

Perhaps the candidate communicates: "$150K is what I am looking for, but I have a $95K base salary now and I don't want to go backward in salary." There should be no surprises when you offer a pay plan to a candidate.

In the early 1990s I learned how to present a pay plan that will likely be accepted by watching one of my very first clients present pay plans to my candidates. I sat in on several presentations from John Lance who was the owner of John Lance Ford in Westlake, Ohio. Lance later sold his large Ford dealership to AutoNation and went on to become a very important executive with AutoNation.

Lance summarized all the aspects of the offer on a sheet of paper for the candidates. In addition to the normal title, hours and salary, Mr. Lance would break down the variable to make it clear to the candidate what they might expect. Over the years I added to this presentation to include 3 levels of performance and 3 possible incomes they would yield. Without this information, I found that candidates often didn't understand, or worse misunderstood, the variable and would often plug in the wrong numbers based on their current position. Once a candidate makes this mistake and comes up with the wrong numbers and talks to their spouse, it becomes very difficult to change their thinking. Especially if you have to also change the spouse's thinking.

Here is our formula to present a pay plan that will get accepted:

- Title

- Duties/Responsibilities/Authority

- Expected start date

- Days/Hours of work

- Exempt or non-exempt

- Paid time off

- Benefits begin

- Other

- Base salary or hourly wage

- Variable/bonuses/commissions based on ....(example: Line T7406 of the Toyota Service DOC)

  > **Underperform**: If your work produces no change from company's performance last year, your variable compensation will be $_____

  > **Perform at target**: We are looking for a 10% increase in performance (sales, profit, etc.) and your variable compensation will be $_____

> **Perform above target**: Reach a 15% increase in performance (sales, profit, etc.) and your variable compensation will be $_____

I encourage my clients to use a presentation like this to make it crystal clear what the candidate can expect. Note, I have found high-performers always feel that they will be "above target range." Many ask what will a 20% improvement pay them?

An added plus with this pay plan presentation is that the majority of your offer letter is mostly written!

Case Study: Collection Manager offer by phone

Our client was a regional automotive finance company in the Midwest. They were hiring a new collection manager to replace their underperforming collection manager. We used our trial closes throughout the interviewing process for each candidate making sure that we were all on the same page. When our client called us to tell us which of the candidates they had chosen, we complimented their choice and let them know that we would make the offer for them.

Now we had to learn the specific compensation plan to make an intelligent offer and answer the anticipated questions. Throughout the process, we also communicated salary, variable income, and time off requirements each of the candidates had communicated to us. Our client already knew what the offer had to be for it to be accepted. Our client gave us the usual salary plus bonus plan plus days off and benefits. However there was not enough information to show the candidate what that would yield.

When I asked them a standard question about what the variable will be with no production increase, a 10% increase as targeted, and over-performing at 15%, they did not know. Not knowing will allow for misunderstandings to creep in and the candidate either needing more salary or passing on the position entirely. I asked them to get back with me with the information. From time to time, clients get nettled when asked for this detailed information. We have to massage their feelings sometimes, but we need the information to make a professional presentation on their behalf.

When I called the candidate to make the offer, I already knew what the candidate was looking for from our trial closes.

Remember our trial closes?

"Did anything change on your end?"

"OK, still interested?"

"Great, the offer we are thinking here is:

> Title of position is Collection Manager:

> Duties / Responsibilities and authority:

> Salary of.........

> Variable of ....

The offer follows the same format.

Great news Jill! XYZ Corporation wants you to be their Collection Manager...

Allow time here for congratulations and human interaction.

"Jill, you and I have discussed what you are looking for to accept this position and I communicated it to XYZ Corporation. I think that they have met everything that you required."

> Title of position is: Collection Manager

> Duties /Responsibilities and authority

> Start date of: usually 2 weeks out (can be much longer for executive positions)

> Days and hours of work

> Position is exempt

> 3 weeks' vacation starting 6 months after your start date

> Benefits begin 30 days after start date

> Other ....''

"Jill, Let's break down the variable."

"If you do not make any improvements, your bonus would be $4,000."

"With a targeted 10% improvement, XYZ Corporation is expecting your bonus will be $20,000."

"If you outperform target and have 15% improvement, your bonus will be $30,000."

"Does this represent what we discussed?"

If yes, ask if they accept the position?

I like to close the call be summarizing:

"Jill, then can I call (representative from the company) and let them know that you are accepting the position:

> With the title of: Collection Manager

> Start date of: specific date

> Days and hours

> Position is exempt

> Base salary of: $80,000

> Bonus: as discussed

> 3 weeks' vacation starting 6 months after your start date

> Other if there is anything else

"Yes you can" is the only answer that you are looking for. "Congratulations!!!"

What I want you to understand is that there should be a formalized structure to your offer so that you dot your "I"s and cross your "T"s. Everything is communicated accurately giving the candidate comfort that they understand the offer and reducing the possibilities of the dreaded misunderstandings. You will also feel more confident presenting an offer this way.

With a large company, I will let the candidate know that someone from Human Resources will reach out to the candidate and send a letter of intent. With smaller companies, without a human resource staff, I often arrange for the candidate to call the hiring manager or business owner to formally accept the position and cement the deal. With smaller companies, we often draft the letter of intent and have the company read and approve it before we send it to the candidate.

What to Do if Candidate Rejects Offer

In the real world, it does not always go so smoothly. Bumps arise in the road to the close. If you tested the offer, you should be able to close – if the candidate truly wants your position.

If the candidate did not tell you why they are rejecting the offer — ask. Decide what will it take and whether you are willing to pay the price.

As an example, we have closed many deals where a great candidate initially turned an offer down because they decided the drive was too far. Often, offering a flexible start time can save the day. Even a $100-per-month gas card can be a small price that may make a big difference to get a high-performing employee who is worried about a long drive.

When it is about money, I advise that you be flexible but never make a deal you will not want to live with. This is where doing your homework, intelligent interviewing, and reference-checking will pay off. If you have a terrific candidate, they will always make money for you. Hiring a lesser candidate for lesser money may not be the smart move.

If you really want the candidate, and they just turned down your offer, you can ask: "*Well I thought that we were making a fair offer, but we are open-minded. What is your thinking.*"

If they want your job, they will tell you and you can negotiate.

If they have gone far from what they agreed to in your "test offers," keep the law of Inverse Proportionality in mind. They may not really want your position. So here is what I do in these cases – I will remind the candidate that we discussed "base salary" several times and they communicated that the number was agreeable, then ask: "*What changed?*"

If I think I am being leveraged for them to get a counter-offer, I rescind the offer and move on. From time to time, I hear a reasoning that will make sense and may meet their offer.

Keep in mind that hourly workers such as office support and technical personnel may point out that other companies are paying more — as seen from their job postings – and that is what they want. Your decision is to match or move on. Again this is where your homework on the candidate will pay off!

Chapter 7

PROFESSIONAL ONBOARDING AND POST-HIRE

ONBOARDING IS MORE than new hire orientation. Onboarding helps set a professional tone for the nervous new hire and creates a terrific first-day impression. Over the years, I have seen new hires get started and, on their first day of work, the manager who hired them is off that day or out of the office on business and no one knows about this person getting started. It's not a stretch to think that this new hire will wonder if they made a mistake taking this position. Now imagine this person explaining to their spouse that evening what their first day was like!

Employees who are professionally onboarded are more likely to stay with an organization, which keeps recruiting costs lower and maintains productivity. I have been troubled when I have seen companies treat lower level employees like second class citizens until "they prove themselves." In my experience, this is more common with smaller companies where they do not have proper procedures in place. Many companies do not have a formalized training program, mentoring program or even a program in place to help make sure the new hire will be successful. Many companies wonder why they have such a high turnover rate, especially in their sales department. Contrast this with going to work at a large company – let's say a bank – and seeing the extensive onboarding procedures they have in place for the new hire.

Your onboarding process has to cover the logistics such as briefing on employee benefits, signing any necessary documentation, and where to go. A good onboarding process should also help your new employee learn about company culture, shared mission, and current projects and reassure them that they made a terrific decision going to work here.

Make sure you have the onboarding process organized and friendly. Human Resources staffs may be performing these tasks on a daily basis. This is more challenging for department managers or business owners who do not perform this task regularly. So please take the time to be organized and prepared. We created an extensive checklist to help you. It may be time-consuming, but it is very important to get the onboarding right. This will save you time by not losing a good employee.

Employees you onboard professionally will do the same if they are in a hiring position for your organization. This will help you retain personnel and build a good reputation for future candidates.

The onboarding checklist we recommend includes:

Prior to the first day:

- Where to go for 1st day including address.

- Who to ask for — and make sure that person is prepared to do their part.

- Time to arrive.

- Parking arrangements.

- Acceptable attire.

- Lunch protocol.

- Cultural tips that may be unique to workplace.

- How and when pay is distributed.

- Details about any paperwork they need to bring or will be filling out their 1st day.

- Any identification they need to bring such as a driver's license or state identification card.

The day your new hire starts:

- Introduce your new team member.

- Show your new hire where everything is – bathrooms, lunch rooms, meeting rooms, their work area, etc.

- Assign a mentor to help the person get settled.

- Make sure the new hire has all that is needed to perform duties successfully.

- Start their training program.

30 days after new hire starts:

- Have a manager get an update on how things are working out.

- Is the work content what they had expected.

- Address any issues with the new hire.

- Ask how the process could be improved.

KEEPING YOUR PERSONNEL

In this book we have discussed the difference in Job Seekers and Career Seekers. The same is true when they become employees. There are job-oriented and career-oriented employees. Both types are needed for an organization to prosper. Executives are usually career-oriented. For the non-executive employees, you will have those who are job-oriented and those who are career-oriented. High-performing employees tend to be career-oriented. Although there are higher performing employees who are not career-ambitious, but are just more conscientious, possess a natural attention to detail, or have developed a strong work ethic or are brighter.

Most high-performing employees want challenge. To keep them engaged and happy, let them know what your expectations are for them to take on additional duties and move up.

Larger companies usually have very formalized steps to take for career advancement. Smaller companies often do not. As an example, large financial clients of ours will hire someone such as a credit underwriter, (making decisions on approving loans or not approving). Credit underwriters can move to a credit underwriter 2, and then to a senior credit underwriter. After that is a management track such as assistant credit supervisor, credit supervisor, assistant credit manager, credit manager, vice president of credit, director of credit.

The point I want you to keep in mind is why high-performing employees may likely leave your organization — lack of opportunity. Make sure they know what the opportunities are with you. You might ask, what if we are a smaller organization and do not offer such upward mobility? This is very common in small and mid-size companies. Smaller companies are more at risk of losing their high-performers to larger companies. What can you do to engage them for longer periods?

Case Study: How a small finance company kept its highest-performing credit underwriters

A client of ours was, at the time, a 100+ person finance company. They had 6 credit underwriters. Of the 6 credit underwriters, 4 were happy doing their job and not career-ambitious. They were not interested in more duties. However they had 2 high-performing credit underwriters who were at risk of moving to larger finance companies for greater challenge and dollars. This is very common employment math for non-executive positions. Many employees are productive and good workers and fairly happy with that. However, the high-performers need more challenge to stay happy. You need to keep your high-performers!

For the 2 credit underwriters who were more ambitious, we recommended that our client make new titles of senior credit underwriter with more pay and additional duties such as training new credit underwriters. I have noticed over the years that high-performing employees usually take on extra duties such as training and coaching without being asked. It is their nature. This bought them some time and extended the interest of the 2 higher performers. Eventually one moved up to credit manager. However there was "no more up" in that department. That left the other ambitious senior credit underwriter very vulnerable to leaving. We recommended something we thought was both smart and proactive.

They sat down with this senior credit underwriter and let them know that they have identified them as a "high-potential employee." The senior credit underwriter very much liked hearing this. Additionally, they asked the senior credit underwriter if they would like to be crossed-trained in other departments such as collections, recovery and remarketing? As you might expect, the employee liked this idea very much because it appealed to their natural high-performer personality. This person became a manager in several departments and later a vice president.

Keep this in mind for your high-potential employees even when you do not have a higher level opportunity for them. Give them more duties, more pay, cross-train them. As an example, consider your high-performing sales person who will be sales manager someday, however your sales manager isn't going anywhere for a while (you hope). Give this high-performing sales person the title senior sales representative or assistant sales manager. Add extra duties such as training new sales personnel, helping close troubled deals, and some extra pay. You will be accomplishing several things. You will keep this high-performing salesperson interested longer, build bench strength and groom this person for sales manager if your sales manager gets promoted or leaves. Additionally, from my experience, a high-performing sales person may get bored, productivity declines, etc. You have seen this yourself. Now give them some people to train and coach and they actually re-engage at a higher level!

When to 'Upgrade' to a Better Employee for Your Company?

This book is dedicated to helping you find, interview, assess, and hire the best candidates. However, I have a great deal of experience talking to managers and executives who are feeling anxiety about possibly terminating an under-performing employee. When a client calls me and wants to talk about this, I will spend as much time listening as they need. I know the angst they are feeling. They often need to talk to someone to get some moral support. This is a decision that every leader has to make from time to time — when to "upgrade to a better employee."

This is often a difficult decision because it means that an employee will likely be terminated or demoted. The executive knows the disruption this can cause a person. However, a leader has to see the big picture and make decisions that are best for the organization. This is why we say it is lonely at the top. It sometimes is very lonely. So the question is, when do you upgrade to a better employee? Thirty plus years of personnel recruitment has taught us that the wrong answer is: "When a better person comes along!" That is leaving the success of the position to chance or fate, not smart management.

The right answer can depend on circumstances, but a general guideline is that you should consider "upgrading" when an employee is incapable or unwilling to perform up to the company's needs. Insubordination, disruptive behavior, stealing, bad personal habits are other common reasons that employees are terminated.

During good times when business is strong, managers often overlook a "weak link" on their staff. In good times, an underachiever's workload is often spread among others to help. In lean times, staffs are stretched and the underachievers' performances tend to stick out and can bring a department down.

Before replacing an employee, I advise our clients to use a checklist that covers these points Dues the employee:

- Need more training?

- Better oversight?

- A mentor to work with?

- More support?

Do you have the ability to provide these, if needed?

More Training: Frequently, you have a good employee who wants to perform well and has the abilities, but they need more training. Often this training can be facilitated by a fellow employee with more experience. You may be able to have the employee trained while on the job with a seasoned employee. An ancillary benefit is that this helps the person doing the training too.

Sometimes a person can enroll in an online class to address specific needs. Is there a training company, seminar, etc., that you can send the employee to for additional training?

My goal for employees is being "Brilliant at the Basics."

Better Oversight: Is the underachieving employee aware of their "status" as underachieving? Do they know specifically what to do to fix the problem? Many employees are aware that they are not performing up to expectations but do not know what changes to make to correct the problem. They want to perform well, but they need help.

Employees like to have clear objectives and goals. Tracking of their goals and reporting to the employee is very helpful and a standard management practice. However, many managers get too busy and do not give employees the attention they may need. Large companies have formalized structures such as quarterly meetings and annual reviews. Small companies and startup companies seldom have such structure. From my experience, owners of small businesses and department heads find it a distraction to their day to help underperforming employees. Best if you can delegate this to an employee who may like helping a co-worker if you do not.

Here is a great example of Oversight: An automotive finance company we work with has an extensive branch network. They have a great deal of experience helping underperforming branch managers get back on track. I want to share their wisdom with you. When a branch manager is underperforming, they put them on a 4-part, 90-day plan.

1. They assess where the manager is underperforming and communicate this to the manager.

2. Lay out the plan for what needs to be done to correct the issue(s).

3. A regional manager will take responsibility for helping the branch manager.

4. Every 30 days, the branch manager's performance is accessed and communicated back to them.

This is fair to the manager and allows the manager to make adjustments. With such oversight, most managers can correct course and those who cannot are not surprised if they are terminated.

A Mentor: Sometimes a seasoned employee can formally or informally mentor an employee. Mentoring often helps the mentor as much as the student. The old saying is *"the best way to really learn a subject is to teach it."*

Is there a person on staff who can take a role in helping the employee? Many employees who aspire to a management position often like to mentor other employees.

Most of the top leaders I know like to put most of their time into mentoring their "Star" employees. They want to be fair to those who are falling behind. However, as a leader, your time may be best used supporting the high-performers. Most top leaders do not like to spend much of their time with those who are always behind. Business is tough and not everyone is suited to your work. Delegate this task to someone who would enjoy it.

More Support: Does the employee need more support by the company? Better equipment, daily meetings, newer software, additional staff? Perhaps the employee needs to better understand the big picture and how their work fits into this big picture. Does the employee need to get out and go on a sales call, repair call, or attend trade shows? Are there industry periodicals that would help the person?

Time to upgrade

When these are exhausted, it may be time to consider upgrading to a better employee.

I see many executives who should replace a manager who is in "over their head" or has personal issues that are hurting their performance and affecting other employees and, of course, the company's bottom-line!

A president of a subprime automotive finance company taught me his philosophy. He explained that if a person is not a strong fit in his company, he will move them out quickly. This, he explained, has several benefits. First it gives another person the opportunity to excel in the position. Secondly, it gives the terminated employee the opportunity to find a position that they are better suited to so that they too have an opportunity to excel. Additionally the staff will not be negatively impacted by the underachiever.

When dealing with my employees, I keep this in mind: Be firm, kind, and consistent when making such choices. But remember, it is lonely at the top and tough decisions sometimes need to be made.

FIVE THINGS A NEWLY HIRED EXECUTIVE NEEDS TO ESTABLISH

As a veteran of 30+ years of executive search, I have formed an opinion on what a newly hired executive or department head needs to establish very early on. I have observed many very good leaders get started in their new roles, from supervisors to department heads to corporate CEOs. It became clear that some leaders instinctively know how to start off their introduction and lay out their vision, philosophy, corporate agenda and quickly get everyone on board. I want to share what I have observed from these leaders with you.

I was reminded of these aspects while I was watching Jimmy Haslam, the owner of my football team — the Cleveland Browns, during his introductory press conference. He "owned the room " as they say in media. He communicated his vision in 7 words – "Bringing a winning culture back to Cleveland."

From my TV screen, his enthusiasm was palpable and his vision could not be clearer. His philosophy was conveyed to a win-starved fan base – "Steeler football." We all cheered his ownership. I knew I was watching a very seasoned and very good executive at work. Mr. Haslam learned some very painful lessons while becoming a good NFL owner. Like all good executives he did learn.

1. **Vision** – What is the executive's vision of the company/department — its direction. "Here is where we are going together."

2. **Philosophy** – "Tell us the principles by which will you be leading us." Corporate ethics - Values - Aggressiveness - How will we treat employees?

3. **Energy** – The leader sets the pace.

4. **Accountability** – All employees must know what they will be held accountable for, as well as how and when they will be judged on their work product.

5. **Pick great subordinates** - No leader is successful if they do not pick a great support team. I have noticed that the great leaders keep a file of people who impress them and why. They attend conferences and take the time to meet good people and keep a record of them. They spend a lot of time recruiting the best people for their team. They do not just "hire who they already know."

As a leader, I am sure you have your own list of what a new leader needs to establish. I would enjoy hearing what's on your list!

Let's Keep You out of Court

You can be ever so vigilant conducting your own interviews to make sure that you do not ask any illegal questions. However, the odds of a legal issue change markedly when employees of yours begin to interview candidates.

Stay out of court and leave the lawyers on the golf course by teaching your employees the most common illegal questions and the ways to avoid them. I will provide a list here for you to make it much easier for you to teach people interviewing for you. Every new employee you hire who will be in a position of hiring should read it and sign a copy acknowledging it when they first join your organization. If you do not interview candidates regularly, you may want to review this list prior to any interviewing.

It is your responsibility to make sure you nor any of your employees ask any questions that can lead to legal issues. The problem is that many of the "out of bounds questions" seem harmless but have led to million-dollar lawsuits. Questions to avoid generally inquire about:

- Age
- Family
- Gender
- Sexual orientation
- Marriage
- Nationality/race
- Religion
- Political affiliation

Salary history questions. In addition to the above, please keep in mind that a number of state and local legislators, including those in California and New York City, are moving to ban questions about job candidates' salary histories. As of this writing, this is a fluid situation and you should discuss this with a local attorney, at the minimum Google a current list to see what is appropriate where you are hiring.

The following employment laws should be familiar to all personnel who conduct interviews for your organization.

Equal Employment Opportunity

Equal employment opportunity laws cover the rights of all people to work and advance on the basis of merit, ability, and potential. During the 1960s, the federal government and state governments made it illegal to discriminate on the basis of race, religion, sexual orientation, political affiliation, age, race, gender, disability and national origin/ancestry.

You and any employees working for you need to avoid asking questions related to these characteristics.

Title VII Of The Civil Rights Act

Title Vll of the Civil Rights Act states that it is illegal to ask discriminatory questions during the interviewing process regarding the applicant's gender, age, race, national origin, religion, or other non-job-related basis.

Age Discrimination In Employment Act (ADEA)

This act, passed in 1967, prohibits employment discrimination against individuals aged 40 through 69. This act includes failure to hire, discharge, denial of employment, and discrimination with respect to the protected age.

The Americans With Disability Act (ADA)

The ADA protects qualified individuals with disabilities from discrimination in the workplace. The ADA prohibits employers from asking questions about a candidate's physical or mental condition during the interview or application process.

Job-relatedness

To help ensure equality and fairness to any candidate, interviewers need to have a list of job-related interview questions, which are asked consistently for all applicants for the same position. A question not related to job performance should not be asked. The employer must demonstrate a job-related need for questions asked. In the event that you cannot, you then create a possibility that the EEOC could scrutinize your hiring practices and see if discrimination has taken place.

Now that we "know" what not to ask, let's make this abundantly clearer and put it in a much more usable format and keep you and your staff on safe legal grounds!

Nationality and Citizenship

Don't ask:

- *What is your national origin?*

- *Where did your parents come from?*

- *What is your maiden name?*

Try asking this way:

- *Are you legally eligible for employment in the United States?*

- *Have you ever worked under a different name?*

Arrest and Conviction

Don't ask:

- *Have you ever been arrested?*

Try asking this way:

- *In the last 10 years, have you ever been convicted of a crime?*

- *If yes, when and where was the disposition of the case?*

Disabilities

Don't ask:

- *Do you have any job disabilities?*

Try asking this way:

- *Can you perform the duties required of the job?*

Attendance and Scheduling

Don't ask:

- *How many children do you have?*

- *Are you planning to have more children?*

- *Are any of your children preschoolers?*

- *Do you own a car?*

- *What religion are you?*

Try asking this way:

- *What days/hours can you work?*

- *Do you have responsibilities that will interfere with our job requirements such as traveling?*

Credit Record

Don't ask:

- *Do you own your home?*

- *Have your wages ever been garnished?*

- *Did you ever declare bankruptcy?*

Try asking this way:

- This line of questioning you may want to avoid altogether. Keep in mind that credit references can be used in compliance with the Fair Credit Reporting Act of 1970 and with the Consumer Credit Reporting Reform Act of 1996.

Address

Don't ask:

- *Do you own your home?*

- *What was your previous address?*

- *How long did you live there?*

- *How long have you resided at your current address?*

Try asking this way:

- Best to avoid this line of questioning altogether.

Gender Based Questions

Don't ask:

- *Are you a Mr.? Mrs.? Miss? Or Ms?*

Try asking this way:

- Another series of questions best avoided.

Military Record

Don't ask:

- *What type of military discharge did you receive?*

Try asking this way:

- *What type of education, training or work experience did you receive from the military?*

Organizational Affiliations

Don't ask:

- *What societies, clubs, political associations do you belong to?*

Try asking this way:

- *Are there any organizations, that you consider relevant to your ability to perform the position?* Over the years we have heard informative answers to this question such as, I joined Toastmasters to improve my public speaking skills or I am a member of the Society of Actuaries to stay on top of industry best practices.

Religion

Don't ask:

- *What is your religion, church or parish or religious holidays observed?*

Try ask this way:

- Best avoid all questions related to religion.

Workers' Compensation

Don't ask:

- *Did you ever file for workers' compensation?*

- *Do you have any prior work-related injuries?*

Try asking this way:

- These questions again are best avoided.

As you can see, there are certain lines of questioning that you best avoid. There are some questions that you can ask; however, they can be illegal if you ask them the wrong way. As you can see in the questions above, we state some "Don't ask" and "Try asking this way." Please bear in mind that by suggesting that you "try asking this way," is not in any way an attempt to get around the law. It is meant to make sure that neither you nor a member of your staff inadvertently asks a legal question the wrong way. You could offend candidates and lead to very expensive legal issues.

Prep Quiz/Answers

The purpose of this quiz is to test your knowledge of the recruitment process. Take this quiz prior to reading this book and again after reading the book. See how your answers change.

1. The best indicator of a candidate's future performance and success with your organization is:

    a. How well they present themselves during your interview.

    b. They say all the things you were looking to hear.

    c. They have a strong record of successful past performance.

    d. They aced your corporate testing.

2. The best indicator that a sales representative candidate will be a great hire for you is:

    a. They blow you away during the interview.

    b. You toss a stapler in their lap and ask them to "sell it to you" and they do very well selling it to you.

    c. You see a past record of high performance.

    d. They aced your "Profile Assessments."

    e. If they can "sell you" during the interview they will sell to your clients as well.

3. Which point is often overlooked by employers when creating a winning job posting to attract a superior candidate?

    a. Very detailed job description covering the duties and responsibilities of the opportunity.

    b. List of stringent qualifications to ensure the best candidates will apply.

    c.   A description of your company and what a person can accede to in this position.

4. The best method to delegate responsibilities to hiring committees is: (Example is 5 people on hiring committee deciding between 4 candidates interviewed)

    a.   Majority rules.

    b.   Unanimous or keep looking.

    c.   All committee members have a say, but final decision rests with the member who the candidate will report to.

5. When you are interviewing a sales rep or mid-level manager, the best sign that you have a good candidate is:

    a.   Willingness to start right now with you.

    b.   Cautious, asks a lot of questions, needs time to think about it.

    c.   Blows you away during the interview.

6. Which is correct - What a candidate wants from a career move, (candidate's mindset) is:

    a.   Just as important as their education and experience.

    b.   Not your problem and should be left to the candidate to sort out.

7. Which is more reflective of a Career Seeker Vs a Job Seeker?

    a.   They come to your interview enthused and willing to jump through any hoop for you.

    b.   A willingness to commit to your position during first interview.

    c.   Wants time to reflect on your opportunity and where it will lead them.

8. Check each that apply - When interviewing candidates in-person:

☐ You are able to spell out a compelling reason why any candidate should consider leaving their current position to join your company.

☐ You can explain "what the candidate can become" by taking your position.

☐ You tell them about the team they will be joining.

☐ (If candidate is from a different industry), You have compelling reasoning for them joining your industry.

☐ You provide literature for candidate to take home to review and share with spouse/mentor.

9. To save everyone's time, do you prepare a list of "knock-out factors" when beginning a search such as:

› Candidate's ability to commute to your office daily or relocate.

› Non-compete exists that may affect their current employment.

› Specific knowledge necessary such as "EXCEL expertise."

› Needed licensure (driver's license needed to do job, CPA required).

› Credit and criminal background checks needed before offer letter.

› Ability to travel as required.

Please note the question is not **should you**, it is **do you**...?

☐ Yes

☐ No

10. Post interview: Check all which you do regularly in your post interview meeting with your hiring committee:

☐ Assess each candidates' abilities to perform the needed functions of the position.

☐ Ask what concerns exist for each candidate.

☐ Ask how candidate will fit into your corporate culture.

☐ Ask if candidate can duplicate their past success in your position.

☐ Consider what obstacles candidate have in achieving the same level of success with your opportunity.

☐ Discuss what help – training – investment will candidate need from you and can you pay that price.

☐ Does candidate have a compelling reason to take your opportunity.?

☐ What concerns does the candidate have and can you overcome them?

Suggested Answers

Question 1 — Answer is C. In this question we are asking for the "best indicator," not just a positive sign. After 30 years of executive search and following several thousand candidates, it is clear that the best indicator of one's future performance is their past performance. People's behavior follows distinct patterns most of their adult life. If they are a "hard-charger," they will likely be a hard-charger for you. If they were a low-performer in past positions, you are not likely going to turn them into a hard-charger.

Question 2 — Answer is C. The biggest misconception about hiring – especially hiring sales people – is if they "blow you away" in an interview they are going to great selling for you. We have found no positive correlation with blowing you away in an interview and being a day-to-day, bell-to-bell consistent high-performer. They may possess sales talent, but sales is hard work requiring a great deal of self-motivation. After interviewing thousands of sales personnel, (high- through low-performers), we notice that the top sales people certainly possess a lot of energy but they have a very strong work ethic and are very driven. This shows in their past positions.

Question 3 — Answer C is correct. Most job postings are a boring job description and a list of qualifications. They only attract that 5% to 10% of people currently looking at that time. Unless you are a marquee company like Wells Fargo, Ford, Google, etc., you have to tell people who you are, what you do, and what they can become by taking a position with you. The best candidates are not looking for a "lateral move" they want a position and a company that will enhance their career.

Question 4 — Answer C is correct. I have a long-winded philosophy on this, but keep these points in mind. One person will be managing the new hire and that person needs to take ownership of the hire. I have frequently seen other committee members vote down a very strong candidate because they felt threatened by the candidate's experience, education, drive etc. " Majority rules" and "unanimous or keep looking" often provided for vanilla hires. This is counterintuitive and many managers make this mistake throughout their careers.

Question 5 — Correct answer is B. I have seen many sales executives and managers fall into the trap of hiring a candidate who "blows them away" only to see the sales rep fizzle in the field. Wanting to start right away means they are looking for a job, not a career – bad sign. The best sales reps are smart thinkers and will only move for a better opportunity and will need time to review your opportunity – a good sign even though it is counterintuitive.

Question 6 — Correct answer is A. In the past 30 years, most calls to us come from people who are doing very well, in a good position with a good company. However, the position is lacking something such as interesting day-to-day work content or career opportunity. The superior candidates are looking to increase their knowledge, challenge themselves, take on more responsibility, etc. Learn what your top candidates are looking for and show them how that can be met with your position.

Question 7 — Correct answer is C. A Job Seeker is looking for a job now and will jump through any hoop and commit to a position very early on. They are likely to leave you just as easily in 6 to 12 months! A Career Seeker is looking for career growth and will take time to reflect on your position and company, talk to a mentor and want more information. Give it to them!

Question 8 — I hope you checked all. You should be able to tell the candidate about your industry, company, and specific opportunity and where this can take them. Candidates should research your company on the internet and call colleagues to learn about your position to prepare for the 1st interview. However you know your company much better and you need to "connect the dots" for them and put your opportunity in a positive light. You need to do this to attract the best candidates — assume your completion will be!

Question 9 — Correct answer is Yes. Preparing a list of knockout factors will save you time, aggravation and professional embarrassment. I know of a search a company, (not us), retained to help their client find a CFO. They met a candidate they really liked, had multiple interviews, met with members of the Board of Directors and important investors, negotiated an extensive and detailed employee agreement only to find that the CFO had a non-compete that his current company wasn't going to let him out of! Yikes, heads rolled on that one. We always asked upfront if there is a non-compete and I want you to also ask this.

Question 10 — Answer is all. Take the time to meet with the hiring committee members. Don't just ask who they like best. Take the time to figure out if candidate will fit into your culture. Are your processes similar enough to help the candidate succeed or will they impede their success? What will be the cost to get each candidate "up to speed," who will be responsible, and how long will it take?

EPILOGUE

I WANT YOUR career to soar. Whether you are a small business owner, a corporate department head, Human Resource staff, or corporate CEO, you will be measured by the success of your team. In this book, I have endeavored to share what we have learned in 30 years of recruiting at all levels of positions throughout the United States. I have attempted to teach you the same system we have developed at my firm. I want you to be armed with the ability to find, recruit, assess, and keep the best personnel for your team.

If you follow our proven system, you will be armed with the tools and techniques needed to fill the void in an Ivy League MBA. Have confidence in this system, which is responsible for several thousand successful placements in various industries. Take the time to learn and follow each step. Do not short-cut the process. By building a great team, your career will soar and you will sleep better at night knowing that you can fill any position, no matter how challenging or important.

I want to thank you for the opportunity to guide you and share our 30 years of experience. I also want to thank all the clients and candidates who put their trust in us. Additionally, I want to thank the recruiters who have worked for us over the years — my teammates. I also want to thank the very successful clients who have mentored and counseled me over the years. You have taught me so much and it is an honor to be able to memorialize this and share it with generations to come. This book is for today's and tomorrow's leaders who will be tasked with hiring and building their teams.

CPSIA information can be obtained
at www.ICGtesting.com
Printed in the USA
LVHW011144111119
636963LV00002B/436/P

9 781700 527189